desert ARCHITECTURE

desert

Michelle Galindo

ARCHITECTURE

BRAUN

CONTENTS
ÍNDICE
INHALT
SOMMAIRE

PREFACE

While a desert location may seem extreme to most, architects tend to find this sort of environment rather inspirational. The harsh climate provides opportunities to use natural energies such as solar radiation and night ventilation, which among others play an important role in preliminary planning. These dry regions have been neglected in the past; thought of as a space that can only be conquered by those of us who can endure extreme climatic conditions. However, as our world changes in every aspect, from technological advancements to environmental deterioration, so to will our habitual needs. As estimated, the Earth today is at a growth rate of nearly 80 million people each year, which means that by 2050, humans would add up to the staggering number of 10 billion people. This statistic has called, and in-fact demanded for new and innovative developments, and architects have taken it upon themselves to act as pioneers of this generation to tackle the extreme, and start designing where not many have dared venture.

The intensive desert location is one environment that has provided a solution to escape the overcrowded, increasingly over-populated centers of many countries on our tiny planet. The architects and their work featured in this book are a continuation of the mid-century desert architecture of John Lautner, Richard Neutra and Albert Frey that were inspired by the starkness and the beauty of the desert, and made Palms Springs, California their architectural playground, giving birth to Desert Modernism. The architects of today such as, Richärd+Bauer, Snøhetta, Foster + Partners, Marmol Radziner and Associates, and Rick Joy Architects are recognized in this particular work of art, creating well known projects such as, Desert Broom Public Library in Cave Creek, Arizona, Ras Al-Khaimah-Gateway Project in the United Arab Emirates, Spaceport America in Upham, New Mexico, Desert House in Palm Springs, California and Desert Nomad House in Tucson, Arizona respectively.

These contemporary practitioners approach the hottest biome on earth and land of extremes – 100 degrees Fahrenheit / 38 Celsius during the day to 32 degrees Fahrenheit / zero Celsius at night – with the use of glass, weathered steel, rammed earth, a combination of natural and manmade materials to create innovative spaces and to conquer the desolate drama of the desert coalesce.

Our global awareness is ever changing in regards to what will happen to our world if we do not start to live in a more sustainable manner with a mentality of a more "green" approach. Human behavior has created an imbalance in the atmosphere's carbon dioxide, the Earth's average temperature, and the extraordinary size of the human population. As a direct result from human activity, we have seen pollution effect cities, ice shelves collapsing in Antarctic, rain-forests destroyed around the globe, and global warming becoming a daily discussion not only in G8 Summits, but at home as well. How long before we all start thinking in an extreme fashion about sustainable living? Architects hold this power in their hands, and each one brings a unique and different approach to the way they believe a space should be built in order to be comfortable, sustainable, and habitable. The following architects and work displayed in this volume of architecture in an extreme environment is just the beginning of a phase that is rapidly growing into a worldwide phenomenon. While the buildings and structures possess quality, distinctiveness, and radical characteristics, it is the designers behind the curtain who display genuine innovation in not only trying to make this world a more ecological place to live, but to motivate others to follow in the same direction.

PREFACIO

Si bien para la mayoría un paraje desértico sería extremadamente severo, este entorno suele servir a los arquitectos de fuente de inspiración. Un clima tan riguroso fomenta el uso de fuentes naturales de energía tales como la radiación solar o la ventilación nocturna, uso que, entre otros factores, desempeña un papel fundamental en el planeamiento preliminar. En el pasado, a estos secadales no se les prestó la atención debida, pues se consideraban áreas solo aptas para los más intrépidos capaces de soportar condiciones climáticas extremas. No obstante, el mundo va cambiando en todos los sentidos, desde los avances tecnológicos al deterioro medioambiental; del mismo modo cambiarán nuestras necesidades cotidianas. Se calcula que el crecimiento anual de la población del planeta se sitúa en torno a los 80 millones de personas, lo que significa que en el 2050, la población mundial alcanzará la sorprendente clfra de 10.000 mlllones. Estas estadisticas hacen pensar en nuevas formas de urbanización; de hecho, son una exigencia. Los arquitectos han asumido la responsabilidad y, con ella, el papel de pioneros de esta generación que hará frente a estos excesos, para comenzar a diseñar allí donde muchos ni se aventurarían.

Los intensos parajes desérticos son uno de los entornos que se presentan como alternativa factible a los centros urbanos de muchos países de nuestro diminuto planeta, centros con una superpoblación en continuo aumento. Los arquitectos reunidos en este volumen, junto a sus obras, representan la continuación de la arquitectura del desierto de mitad del siglo pasado de John Lautner, Richard Neutra y Albert Frey, inspirados por la austeridad y la belleza del desierto, y que convirtieron a la californiana Palm Springs en su mesa de operaciones, dando a luz el "Modernismo del Desierto". Algunos arquitectos actuales, como Richärd+Bauer, Snøhetta, Foster + Partners, Marmol Radziner and Associates o Rick Joy Architects, gozan de reconocimiento en este arte tan particular, respectivamente con creaciones tan afamadas como la Desert Broom Public Library en Cave Creek, Arizona, el proyecto Ras Al-Khaimah-

Gateway en los Emiratos Árabes Unidos, el Spaceport America en Upham, Nuevo México, la Desert House de Palm Springs o la Desert Nomad House en Tucson, Arizona.

Estos profesionales contemporáneos se adentran en los biotopos más cálidos del planeta, en esta tierra de extremos – de los 38ºC de día a los 0ºC de noche – mediante el empleo de vidrio, acero corten, tapial y una combinación de materiales naturales y de facturación humana para crear espacios innovadores y dominar el árido espectáculo que representa la amalgama del desierto.

Nuestra conciencia global está cambiando al reflexionar sobre lo que nos deparará el futuro caso de no comenzar a vivir de forma sostenible y con una mentalidad más "verde". Las prácticas humanas han desequilibrado los niveles de dióxido de carbono atmosférico, la temperatura media de la Tierra y son culpables del desproporcionado tamaño de la población mundial. Resultados directos de la actividad humana son los efectos de la polución en las urbes, el desmoronamiento de los glaciares antárticos, la destrucción de las selvas tropicales y el calentamiento global, tema de discusión habitual no solo en las cumbres del G8, sino en cualquier hogar. ¿Cuánto tiempo ha de pasar hasta que pensemos en un cambio radical que nos lleve a un modo de vida sostenible? Los arquitectos tienen ese poder en sus manos; cada uno de ellos lo pone en práctica de forma muy personal, tal y como conciben la modelación de un espacio para hacerlo confortable, sostenible y habitable. Los arquitectos y las obras que compendia este volumen de arquitectura en un entorno de características extremas representan el inicio de un fenómeno que rápidamente está alcanzando dimensiones globales. Tanto los edificios como las estructuras poseen calidad, distinción y propiedades revolucionarias, pero son los diseñadores los que despliegan un genuino carácter innovador, no solo en su intento por hacer de este mundo un lugar más ecológico en el que vivir, sino también a la hora de motivar a otros para seguir por el mismo camino.

VORWORT

Mit der Veränderung unserer Welt in allen Bereichen – von technologischen Fortschritten bis zur Umweltzerstörung – werden sich auch unsere Wohnbedürfnisse verändern. Laut Schätzungen wächst die Weltbevölkerung derzeitig um 80 Millionen Menschen pro Jahr. Demzufolge würden wir bis zum Jahr 2050 die schwindelerregende Zahl von 10 Milliarden Menschen auf der Erde erreichen. Diese Zahlen verlangen nach neuen, innovativen Entwicklungen im Bereich der Baukunst. Während die karge Landschaft der Wüste auf die meisten Menschen befremdlich wirkt, fühlen sich Architekten von solchen klimatischen Bedingungen in ihrer Arbeit inspiriert. Sie leisten bahnbrechende Pionierarbeit, um Lösungen für diese extremen Voraussetzungen zu finden, und entwickeln Projekte, wo es bisher nicht viele vor ihnen gewagt haben. Aufgrund der herrschenden Umwelteinflüsse kann in der Wüste auf ganz andere Ressourcen bei der Energiegewinnung zurückgegriffen werden. So werden Solarenergie und Nachtventilatoren bei der Bauplanung berücksichtigt, um alle Reserven der Umgebung effizient zu nutzen.

In der Bebauung der unfruchtbaren Landschaft der Wüste findet sich die Lösung, der Überbevölkerung in den städtischen Zentren zu entgehen und mehr Lebensraum auf unserem eng gewordenen Planeten zu schaffen. Die in diesem Buch vorgestellten Arbeiten stellen eine Fortsetzung der Wüstenarchitektur von John Lautner, Richard Neutra und Albert Frey dar. Diese Baumeister ließen sich Mitte des 20. Jahrhunderts von der kargen Schönheit der Wüste inspirieren, machten Palm Springs (Kalifornien) zu ihrer architektonischen Spielwiese und schufen den so genannten „Desert Modernism". Auch die zeitgenössischen Architekten wie Richärd+Bauer, Snøhetta, Foster + Partners, Marmol Radziner & Associates und Rick Joy Architects haben sich in diesem Arbeitsfeld einen Namen gemacht und bekannte Projekte wie die Desert Broom Public Library in Cave Creek (Arizona), das Ras Al-Khaimah-Gateway-Projekt in den Vereinigten Arabischen Emiraten, Spaceport America in Upham (New Mexico), das Desert House in Palm Springs (Kalifornien) oder das Desert Nomad House in Tucson (Arizona) hervorgebracht. Mit 38 Grad Celsius am Tag und 0 Grad Celsius in der Nacht bietet die Wüste eine der extremsten Lebensbedingungen auf der Erde. Um in diesen Gegenden innovative Räume zu kreieren und die spärliche Öde zu erobern, verwenden Architekten eine Kombination aus natürlichen und künstlich geschaffenen Materialien, wie Glas, wettergegerbten Stahl und gestampften Boden.

Stetig verändert sich unser Umweltbewusstsein und wir fragen uns, was aus unserer Welt wird, wenn wir nicht beginnen nachhaltig zu leben, zu bauen und „ökologischer" zu denken. Das menschliche Verhalten hat ein gestörtes Gleichgewicht des Kohlendioxidgehalts in der Atmosphäre erzeugt, die Durchschnittstemperatur der Erde erhöht und ein außergewöhnliches Wachstum der Erdbevölkerung verursacht. Die direkte Auswirkung des menschlichen Handelns erleben wir in der großstädtischen Schadstoffentwicklung, dem Zerbrechen von Eisplatten in der Arktis, der Zerstörung von Regenwäldern weltweit und der fast täglichen Diskussion um die Erderwärmung, nicht nur auf den G8-Gipfeltreffen, sondern auch zu Hause. Wie lange wird es noch dauern, bis wir tiefgreifend über einen umweltverträglichen Lebensstil nachdenken? Architekten halten diese Macht in ihrer Hand, und jeder von ihnen hat seine eigene Herangehens- und Denkweise, wie ein Raum gebaut sein sollte, um komfortabel, umweltverträglich und bewohnbar zu sein. Die folgenden Architekten und ihre in diesem Band vorgestellten Bauwerke in extremen Umgebungen stellen erst den Anfang einer Entwicklung dar, die gerade zu einem weltweiten Phänomen wird.

PRÉFACE

Si le désert peut sembler inhospitalier pour beaucoup, certains architectes voient dans ce type d'environnement une source d'inspiration. Le climat extrême permet l'utilisation d'énergies naturelles, comme le rayonnement solaire et la ventilation nocturne, qui jouent un rôle important dans les avant-projets. Ces régions arides étaient autrefois négligées : on pensait que seules des personnes pouvant supporter des conditions climatiques extrêmes pouvait les conquérir. Cependant les changements que subit notre monde, tant dans les avancées technologiques que dans la détérioration de l'environnement, concerneront également nos besoins courants. Aujourd'hui, on estime que le taux de croissance démographique de la Terre est d'environ 80 millions de personnes par an, ce qui signifie que la population mondiale devrait atteindre le nombre stupéfiant de 10 milliards d'êtres humains d'ici 2050. Cette statistique conduit à considérer, et même à exiger, des développements nouveaux et innovants. Des architectes ont décidé d'être les pionniers de cette génération, de s'attaquer à l'extrême et de concevoir des bâtiments dans des lieux où peu de leurs confrères ont osé s'aventurer.

Les étendues désertiques permettent d'échapper à la surpopulation qui touche de nombreux pays de notre petite planète. Les architectes et les travaux présentés dans cet ouvrage constituent l'héritage des pionniers de l'architecture du désert du milieu du XXème siècle, John Lautner, Richard Neutra et Albert Frey. Ces derniers ont été inspirés par l'austérité et la beauté du désert et ont fait de Palm Springs, en Californie, leur terrain de jeu, donnant naissance au Modernisme du désert. Les architectes d'aujourd'hui, comme Richärd + Bauer, Snøhetta, Foster + Partners, Marmol Radziner and Associates et Rick Joy Architects sont reconnus pour leurs œuvres d'art. Ils sont les créateurs de projets bien connus comme, respectivement, la bibliothèque publique Desert Broom à Cave Creek en Arizona, le projet Gateway à Ras Al-Khaimah aux Emirats arabes unis, le port spatial Spaceport America à Upham au Nouveau Mexique, le projet Desert House à Palm Springs en Californie et le projet Desert Nomad House à Tucson en Arizona.

Ces professionnels allient des matériaux naturels et industriels comme le pisé, le verre et l'acier patinable pour s'attaquer au biome le plus chaud de la Terre et territoire des extrêmes (100 °F / 38 °C la journée et 32 °F / 0 °C la nuit). Ils créent des espaces innovants et partent à la conquête de la désolation du désert.

On ne constatera aucune évolution de la conscience mondiale quant à l'avenir probable de notre planète si nous n'intégrons pas les concepts de durabilité et d'écologie. Le comportement humain a généré un déséquilibre du taux de dioxyde de carbone dans l'atmosphere, de la température moyenne de la Terre et du nombre d'êtres humains. Conséquence directe de l'activité de l'Homme, la pollution affecte les villes, les barrières de glace s'effondrent en Antarctique, les forêts denses équatoriales sont détruites à travers le monde et le réchauffement global est devenu une discussion courante tant lors des sommets du G8, que dans les foyers. Combien de temps faudra-t-il pour que nous commencions tous à envisager radicalement un mode de vie durable ? Ces architectes ont ce pouvoir et chacun véhicule une approche unique et différente du confort, de la durabilité et de l'habitabilité de l'espace. Ces professionnels et les travaux présentés dans ce volume consacré à l'architecture dans un environnement extrême constituent l'avant-garde d'une tendance en passe de devenir rapidement un phénomène mondial. Alors que les constructions et les structures combinent qualité, singularité et radicalité, ce sont les créateurs qui font preuve de réelle innovation et essaient de faire de ce monde un lieu plus écologique tout en incitant leurs semblables à poursuivre le même objectif.

NK'MIP DESERT CULTURAL CENTRE

01

01   Wall made of local soils and concrete

E   **Located in the** most endangered landscape in Canada, the design is a specific response to the building's unique context. This 1,600-acre parcel of land, belonging to the Osoyoos Indian Band, features indoor/outdoor exhibits that honor the Band's history. The desert landscape flows over the building's green roof and is held back by the largest rammed-earth wall in North America. Constructed from local soils mixed with concrete, the wall retains warmth in the winter and allows for substantial thermal mass cooling during the summer.

ES   **Ubicado en el** paisaje más peligroso en Canadá, el diseño es una respuesta específica al contexto único del edificio. Este parcela de tierra de 500 hectarias, pertenece al Grupo Indio de Osoyoos, sus espacios consisten de exposiciones en el interior y exterior que honran la historia del grupo. El paisaje del desierto fluye sobre el tejado verde del edificio y es contenido por la pared más grande formada de tierra en Norteamérica. Construido de tierras locales mixtas con el hormigón, la pared conserva el calor en el invierno y permite enfriamento de la masa sustancial termal durante el verano.

D   **In der am** stärksten gefährdeten Landschaft Kanadas gelegen, nimmt der Entwurf Bezug auf die einzigartige Umgebung. Auf diesem 500 Hektar großen Landstück, das den Osoyoo Indianern gehört, finden Ausstellungen über die Kulturgeschichte dieses Volkes statt. Die Wüstenlandschaft fließt quasi über das begrünte Dach des Gebäudes und wird durch Nordamerikas größte Wand aus gestampftem Erdreich zurückgehalten. Entstanden aus einer Mischung von einheimischer Erde und Beton, speichert diese Wand für den Winter die Wärme und ermöglicht thermische Kühlung im Sommer.

F   **Situé dans le** paysage le plus menacé du Canada, cette architecture est une réponse spécifique au contexte unique du bâtiment. Cette parcelle de terre de 640 hectares, appartenant à la tribu indienne des Osoyoos, comprend des expositions intérieures ou extérieures qui rendent hommage à l'histoire de la tribu. Le paysage du désert flotte au-dessus du toit vert du bâtiment, soutenu par le plus grand mur en pisé d'Amérique du Nord. Construit en terre locale mélangée à du béton, le mur retient la chaleur en hiver et permet de rafraîchir considérablement le bâtiment grâce à sa masse thermique pendant l'été.

CANADA

HOTSON BAKER BONIFACE HADEN ARCHITECTS + URBANISTS

Project City Osoyoos (BC)
Typology Culture
Completion Year 2006
Photos Nic Lehoux

02 Building's context in desert

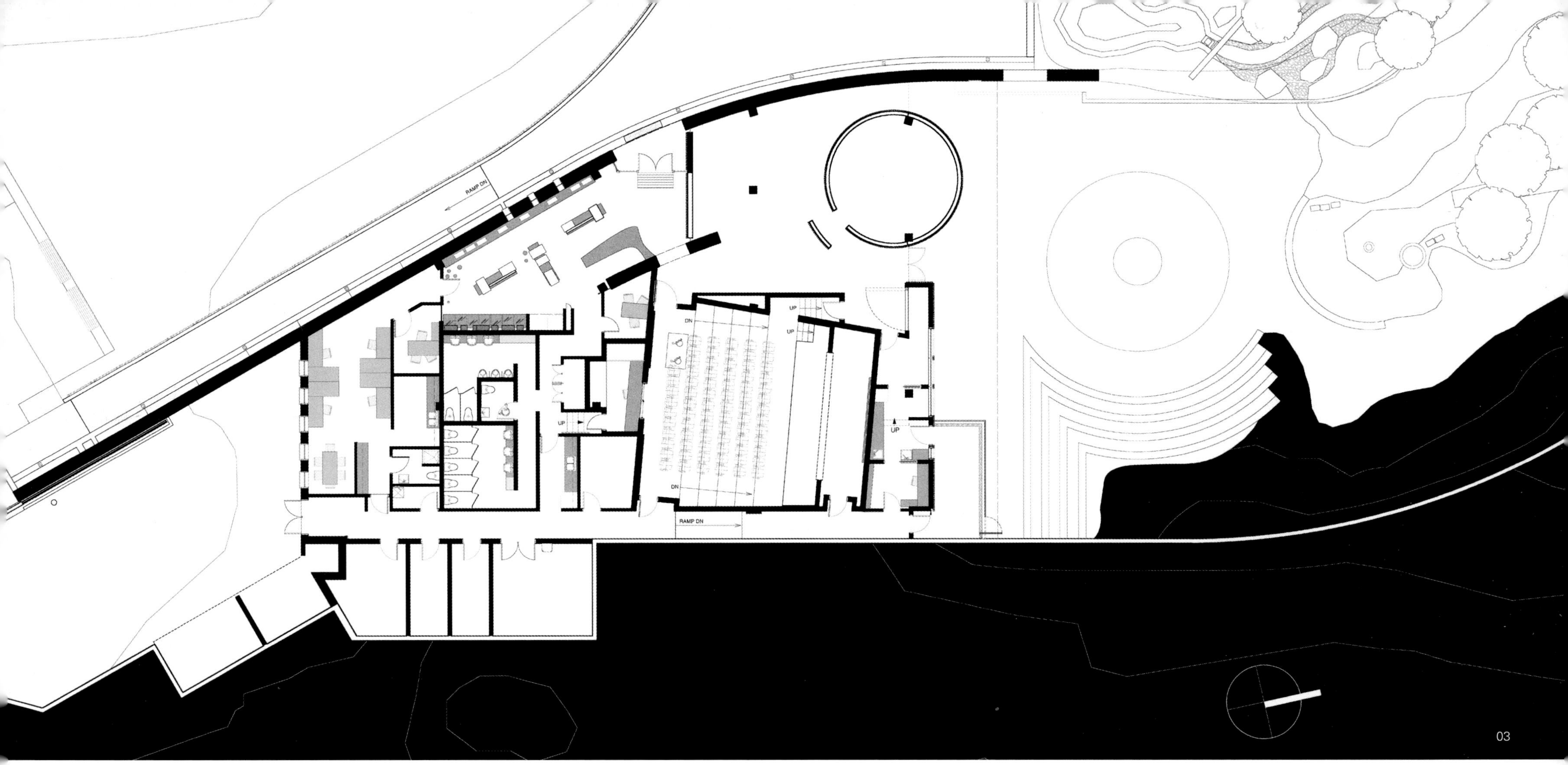

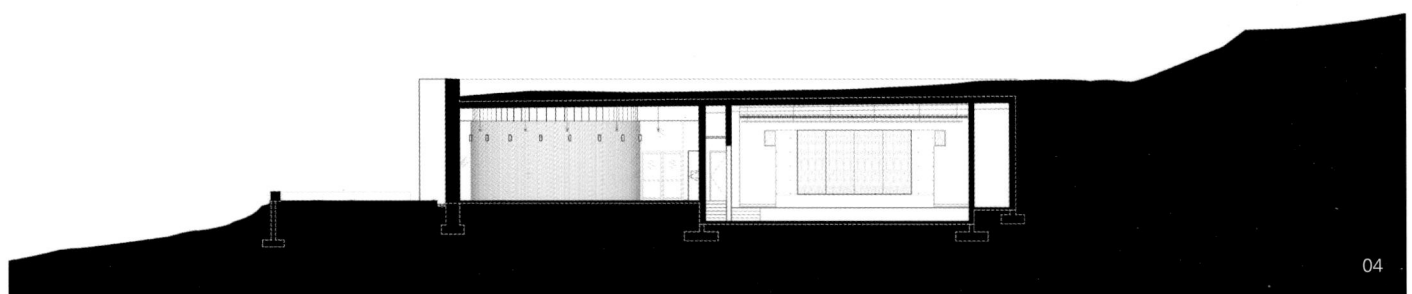

03 Floor plan
04 Section

05 Exterior view
06 Interior view
07 Exterior exhibit of the Osoyoos Indian Band wigwam

05

06

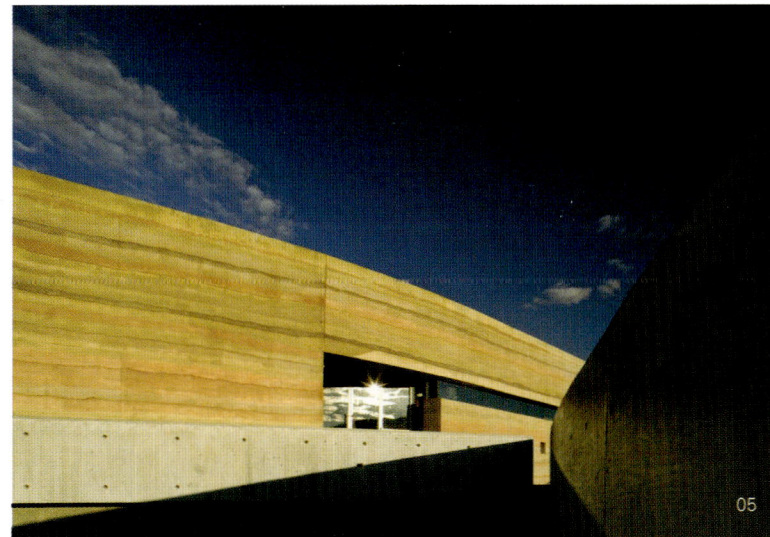

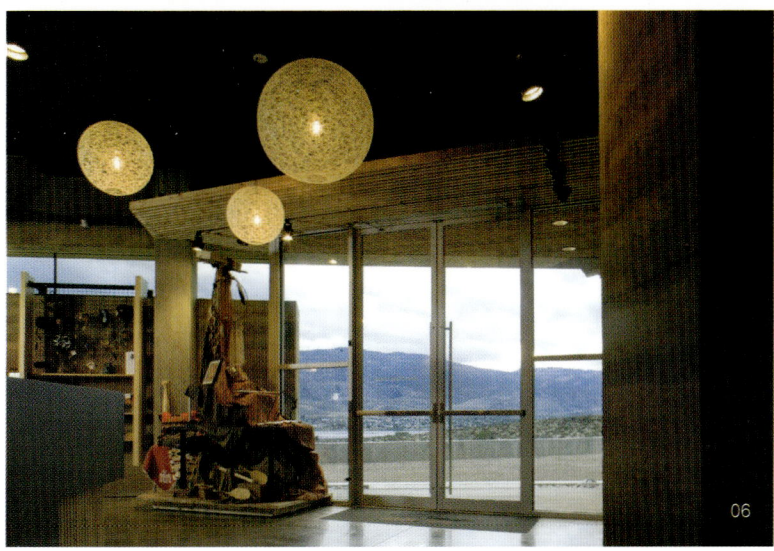

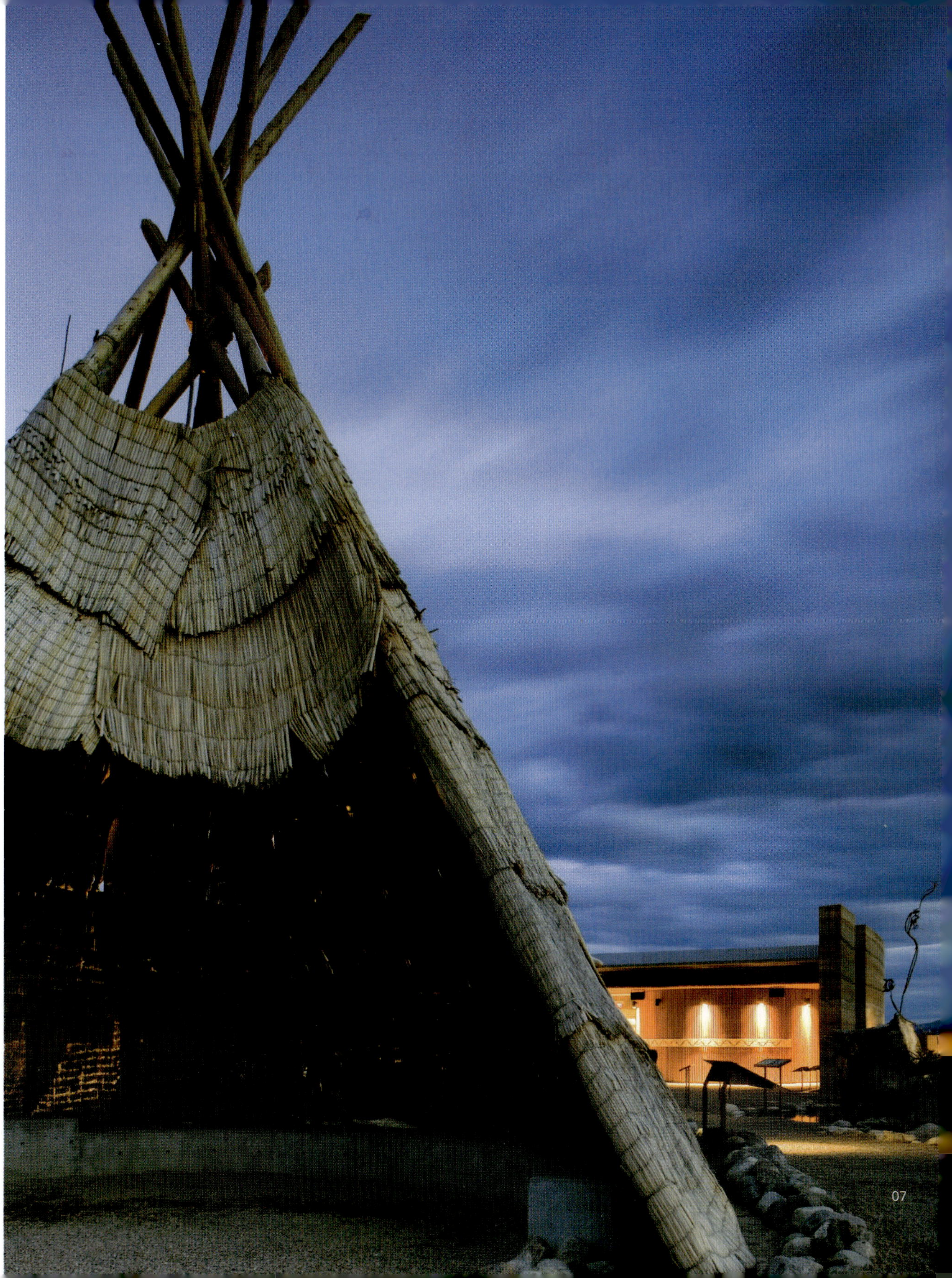
07

SAUNAS AND WATER RESERVOIRES ATACAMA

01

01 Exterior view by night

E **To dwell in** this vast land, men and women build graceful stone structures along the roads in Atacama in order to get an insight into nature, and make it hospitable. These concrete landmarks in the landscape reveal the presence of water reservoirs used to irrigate the land, and allow visitors to swim and to open up new views to the immense wilderness around them. The water is kept still, flowing gently over the reservoir's edges to reflect the light, and the beauty of the place, against a dark slate coating.

ES **Para morar en** esta tierra enorme, los hombres y mujeres construyen estructuras llenas de gracia de piedra a lo largo de los caminos en Atacama para conseguir una perspicacia sobre la naturaleza, y lo hacen hospitalario. Estas señales concretas en el paisaje revelan la presencia de depósitos de agua que solían irrigar la tierra, y permitir a visitantes nadar y abrir nuevas vistas al páramo inmenso alrededor de ellos. El agua se mantiene sin movimiento, fluyendo con cuidado sobre los bordes del depósito para reflejar la luz, y la belleza del lugar, contra una capa de pizarra oscura.

D **Anmutige skulpturale Strukturen** aus Stein an den Straßen von Atacama lassen das unermesslich weite Land wohnlich erscheinen. Diese Bauwerke beherbergen Wasserreservoirs, die zur Bewässerung des Landes dienen und gleichzeitig Besuchern erlauben, schwimmend neue Ausblicke auf die beeindruckende Wildnis zu erlangen. Das Wasser wird ruhig gehalten, es fließt sanft über die Beckenränder. So wirft es das Licht und die Schönheit des Ortes auf die dunkle Schieferbeschichtung zurück.

F **Pour vivre dans** le vaste espace qu'offre le désert d'Atacama, les hommes et les femmes ont construit de gracieuses structures de pierre le long des routes afin de rester connectés à la nature, et de la rendre hospitalière. Ces repères de béton dans le paysage révèlent la présence de réservoirs d'eau pour irriguer la terre, et permettre aux visiteurs de nager et de découvrir une nouvelle vue sur l'immensité sauvage autour d'eux. L'eau reste calme, fluctuant doucement contre les parois revêtues d'ardoise sombre du réservoir pour refléter la lumière et la beauté des lieux.

CHILE

GERMÁN DEL SOL

Project City San Pedro de Atacama
Typology Leisure
Completion Year –
Photos Guy Wenborne

02 View from pool side

03 View from pool to sauna
04 Concrete detail
05 Exterior view by day
06 Transition pools and desert
07 Floor plan, pools

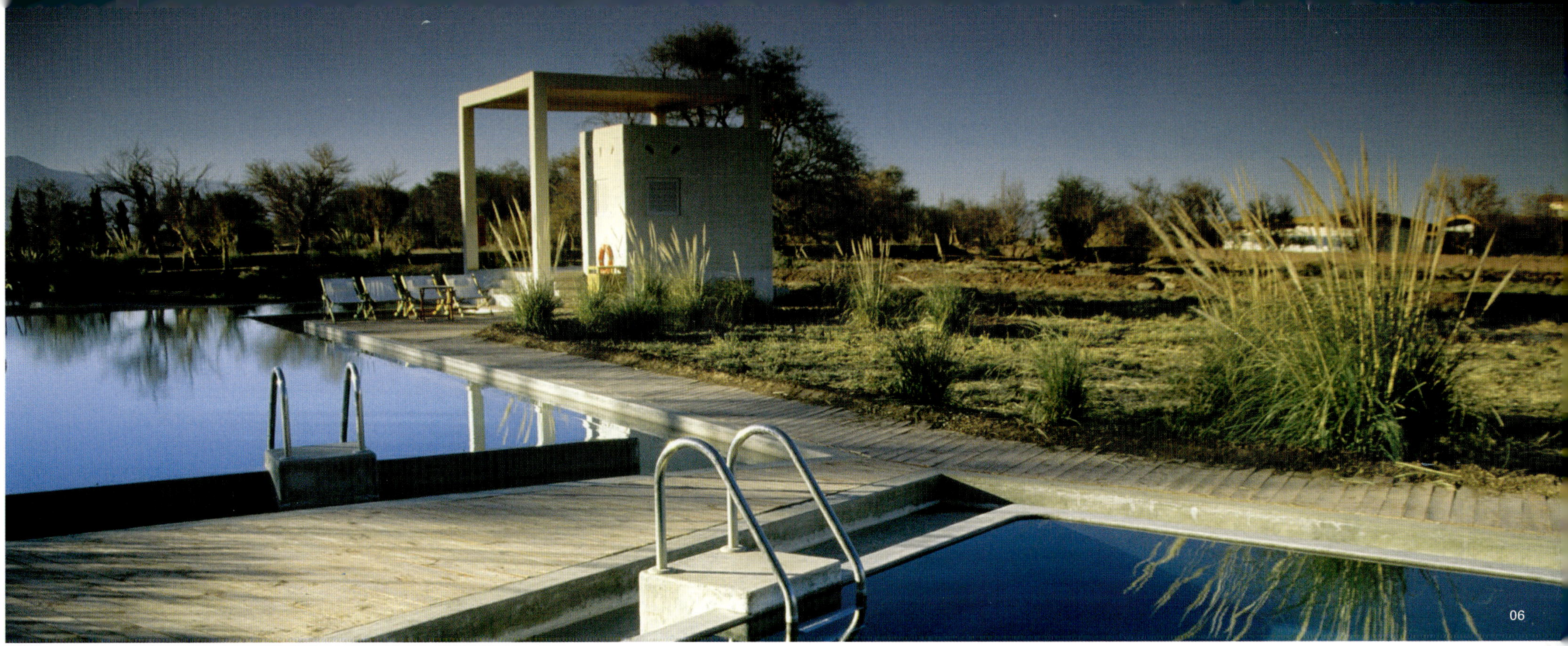

06

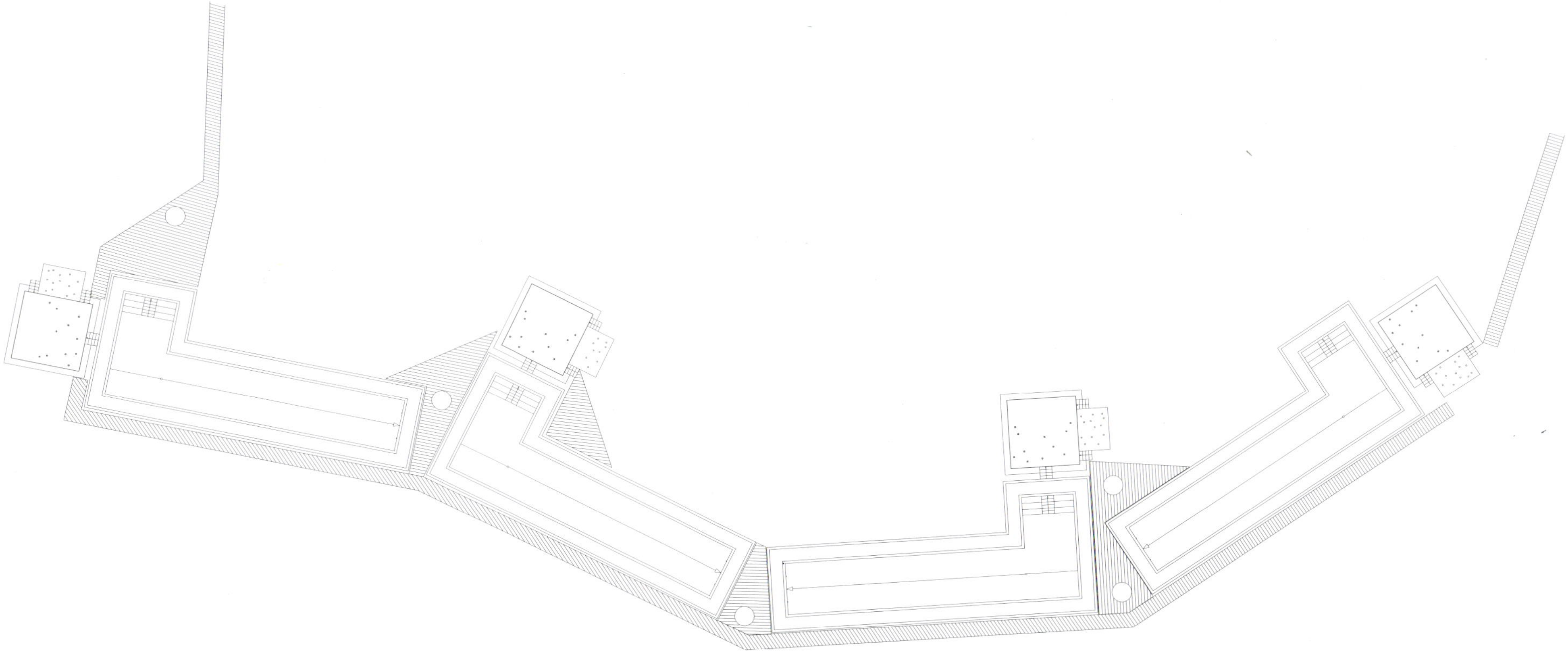

07

HOTEL EN ATACAMA

01   Exterior view, courtyard

E   **Natural and cultural** life, dispersed in Atacama's vastness, is present at the hotel and invites visitors to go out and experience these specific riches. The hotel is distant from existing settlements, and aims to found a new town in Atacama. It follows the pre-Columbian tradition of building in public squares, and creating towns without the use of streets. The building is a sequence of interior and exterior spaces, as is usual in other small towns in Atacama, where the public and the private are not very well defined.

ES   **La vida natural** y cultural, dispersada en la inmensidad de Atacama, está presente en el hotel e invita a visitantes a salir y experimentar esta riqueza específica. El hotel se situa distante de establecimientos existentes, y tiene comom objetivo fundar un nuevo pueblo en Atacama. Siguiendo la tradición precolombina de edificio en plazas públicas, y la creación de ciudades sin el empleo de calles. El edificio es una secuencia de espacios interiores y exteriores, tal cual habituales en otras pequeñas ciudades en Atacama, donde el espacio público y el privado no se definen totalmente.

D   **Das Natur- und** Kulturleben Atacamas ist in diesem Hotel präsent und lädt den Gast ein, den ganz eigenen Reichtum der Region zu erleben. Das Gebäude liegt weit entfernt von den bestehenden Siedlungen und zielt auch darauf ab, eine neue Besiedlung zu gründen. Es folgt der präkolumbianischen Tradition, an öffentlichen Plätzen zu bauen und Städte ohne eigentliche Straßen zu errichten. Der Bau ist eine Abfolge von Innen- und Außenräumen, wodurch das Gemeinschaftliche und das Private nicht streng getrennt sind.

F   **La vie naturelle** et culturelle dispersée dans l'immensité de l'Atacama est présente dans cet hôtel qui invite les visiteurs à sortir et à découvrir ses richesses particulières. L'hôtel est loin des colonies existantes, et vise à fonder une nouvelle ville dans l'Atacama. Il suit la tradition précolombienne du bâtiment sur les places publiques, et de la création de villes sans rues. Le bâtiment est une suite d'espaces intérieurs et extérieurs, comme il est habituel dans d'autres petites villes d'Atacama, où privé et public ne sont pas très bien définis.

CHILE

GERMÁN DEL SOL

Project City San Pedro de Atacama
Typology Hospitality
Completion Year 2006
Photos Felipe Camus (01, 03), Guy Wenborne

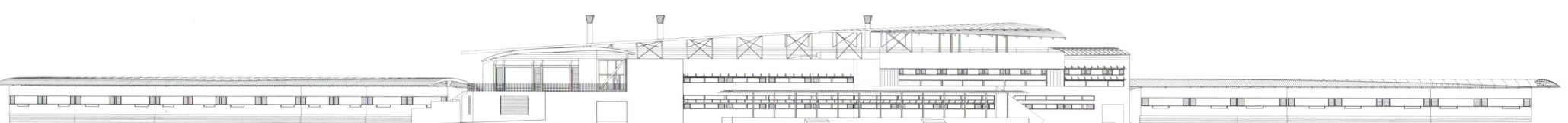

03

04

03 Entry view
04 Elevation
05 Detail entries guest rooms
06 Deck
07 Interior view

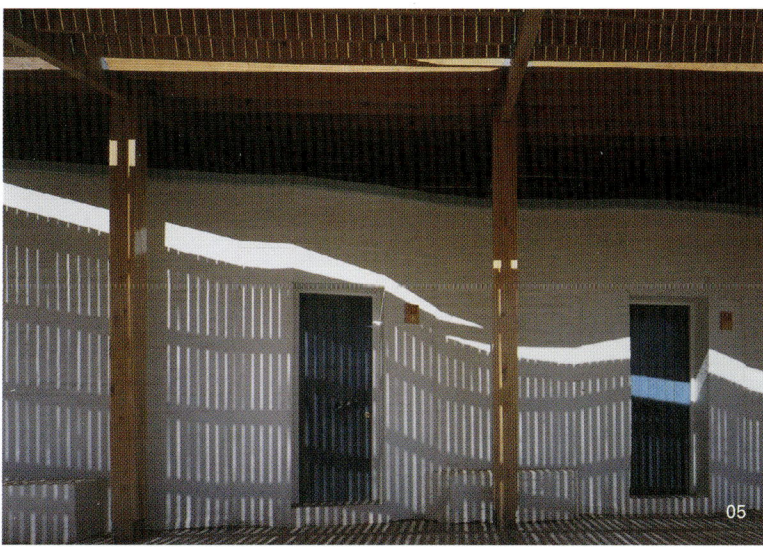

05

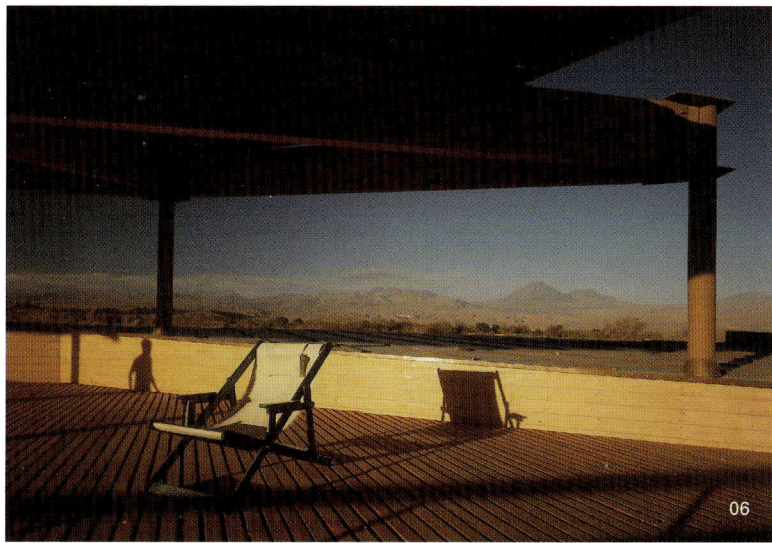

06

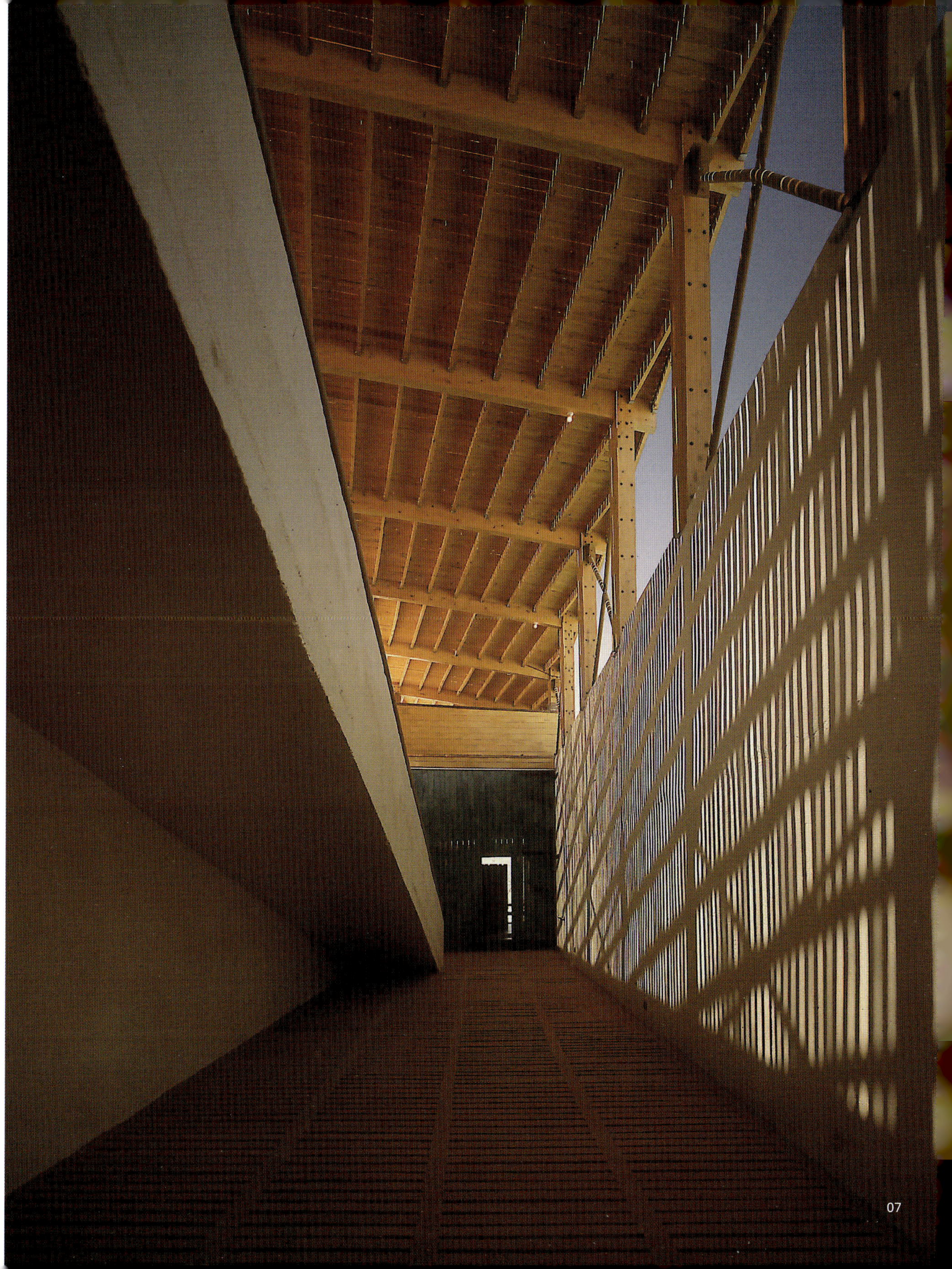
07

TIERRA ATACAMA HOTEL + SPA

01 Exterior view from the pool

E   **The 12 acres** plot, on the outskirts of San Pedro de Atacama with extensive views towards the Lincancabur Volcano was the driving force of the design of this hotel. An ancient bull corral, used years ago to house cattle makes up the entrance with a ramp leading to a 590 feet-long wing. One side of the wing consists of the guest rooms, which form two parallel wings, each having its own terrace, contrasting with the interior and the explosion of light and colors of the desert.

ES   **El solar de** 5 hectarias, en las afueras de San Pedro de Atacama con vistas extensas hacia el Volcan Lincancabur fue el punto de partida del diseño de este hotel. Este se emplaza en lo que había sido un corral de toros de antiguo donde hace años se almacenaba al ganado, convirtiendose ahora en la rampa de entrada principal que guia hacia un volumen de 180 metros de largo. Este volumen aloja las habitaciones en dos alas paralelas, cada una con su propia terraza, creando un contraste con el interior y la explosión de luz y colores del desierto.

D   **Auf einem fünf** Hektar großen Grundstück am Rande von San Pedro de Atacama befindet sich ein altes Bullengehege. Dieser Ort bildet nun den Hoteleingang, von welchem eine Rampe zu einem 180 Meter langen Seitenflügel führt. Die Zimmer, die sich auf einer Seite dieses Flügels befinden, bilden wiederum zwei parallel gelegene Baukörper, die beide mit einer eigenen Terrasse ausgestattet sind. Diese stehen in einem spannungsreichen Verhältnis sowohl zum Interieur als auch zum Licht- und Farbenspiel der Wüste.

F   **Le terrain de** cinq hectares dans la banlieue de San Pedro de Atacama, avec sa large vue sur le volcan de Lincancabur, a été le moteur de la conception de cet hôtel. Un ancien corral à taureaux, utilisé il y a des années pour loger le bétail, en forme l'entrée, avec une rampe menant à une aile de 180 mètres de long. Un côté de l'aile comprend les chambres, qui forment deux ailes parallèles, chacune ayant sa propre terrasse, contrastant avec l'intérieur et l'explosion de lumière et de couleurs du désert.

CHILE

RODRIGO SEARLE Y MATIAS GONZALES

Project City San Pedro de Atacama
Typology Hospitality
Completion Year 2008
Photos Sebastian Sepulveda

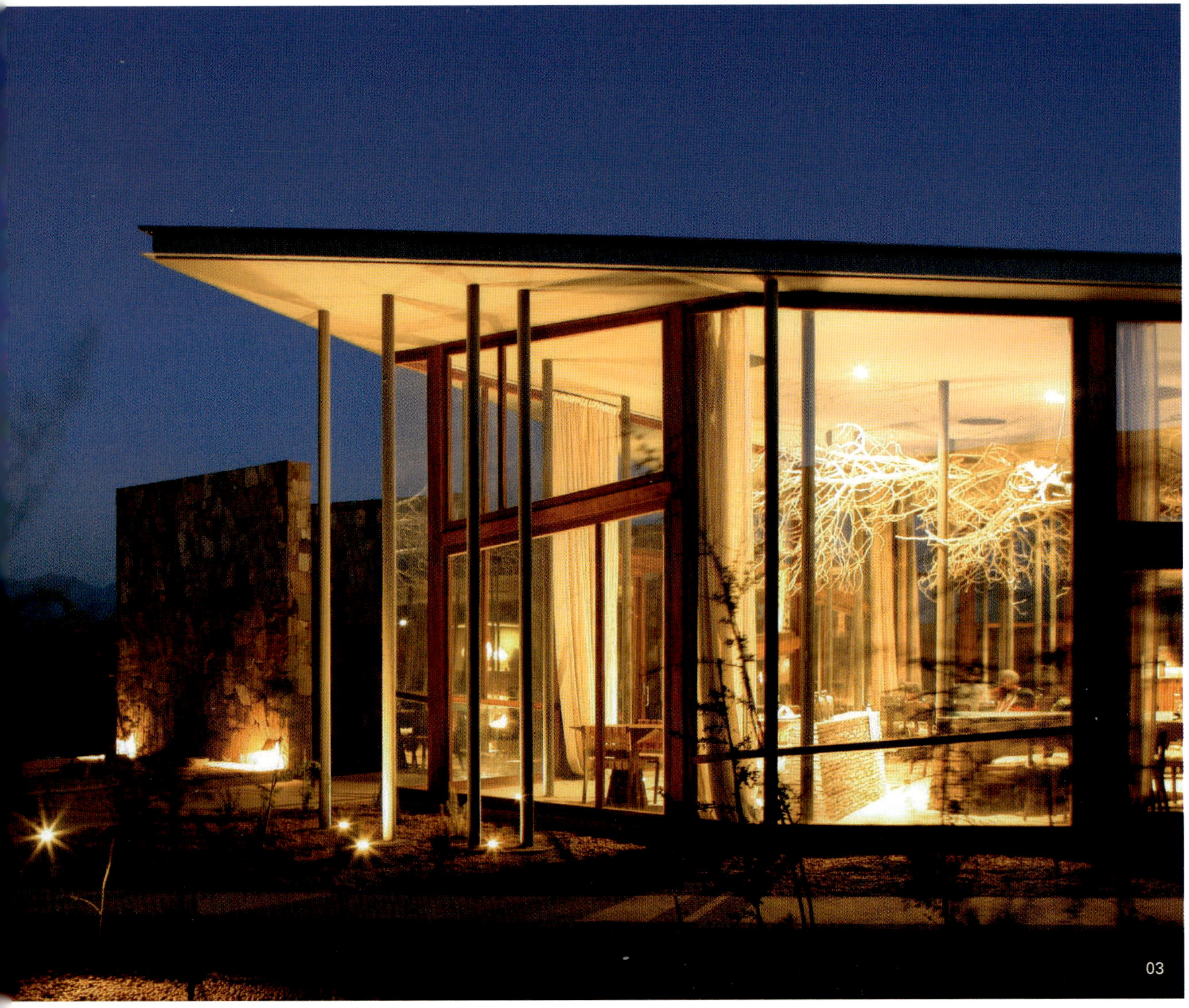

03

04

05

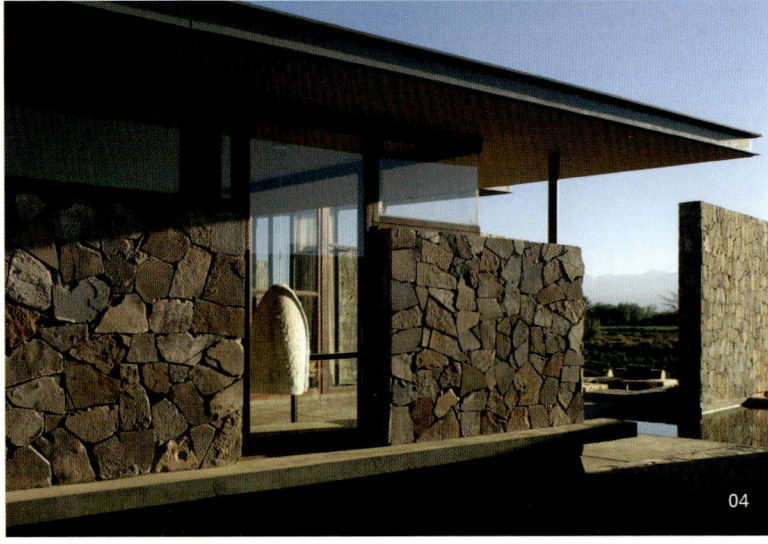

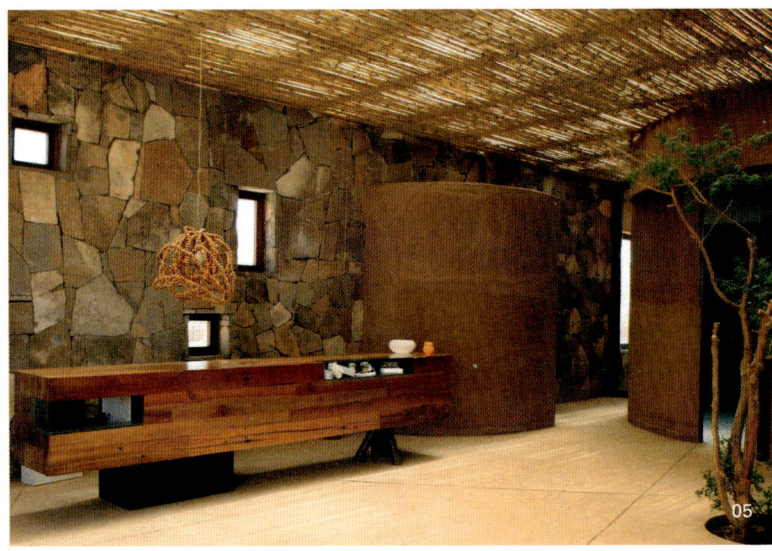

03 Exterior view by night
04 Detail ancient bull corral
05 Interior view, lobby
06 Talabre stone and glass wall
07 Section, east and west room

06

07

CASA GUTHRIE

01

01 Interior view

E   **This house was** commissioned by a real estate firm, which wanted the design of a repeatable house. Situated on a slope with a 25% average gradient, was designed for a newly born family requiring a living area of no more than 1507 square feet. The proposal was a house without a façade being developed from the street level downwards. Casa Guthrie is not just the answer to an issue over a medium gradient site, but a reflection to the real estate system's final target being to sell "attractive" and "good price" houses.

ES   **El encargo de** una inmobiliaria para diseñar una casa repetible capaz de emplazarse en una ladera con una pendiente promedio de un 25%. La casa fue diseñada para una familia incipiente que no requiriera una superficie mayor a los 140 metros cuadrados. La propuesta fue una casa sin fachada, una construcción que se desarrollara desde el nivel de la calle hacia abajo. Casa Guthrie no es sólo la respuesta a un problema de vivienda en un sitio de mediana pendiente, sino una reflexión crítica al sistema inmobiliario cuyo objetivo final es vender casas de "buen gusto" a "buen precio".

D   **Casa Guthrie liegt** an einem schrägen Hang mit einem Neigungsgrad von durchschnittlich 25 Prozent. Die Aufgabenstellung einer Immobilienfirma bestand darin, einen Musterhaustyp zu entwerfen. Für eine junge Familie mit einem Raumbedarf von maximal 140 Quadratmeter errichtet, entstand ein Haus ohne Fassade, das sich vom Straßenniveau her nach unten ausbildet. Das Haus ist nicht nur die Lösung für die besondere Beschaffenheit des Grundstücks, sondern trägt ebenso dem wesentlichen Ziel des Auftraggebers Rechnung, attraktive und preisgünstige Häuser anzubieten.

F   **La commande a** été passée par une société immobilière qui souhaitait une maison à l'architecture reproductible. Conçue pour une jeune famille n'ayant pas besoin de plus de 140 mètres carrés et située sur une pente moyenne de 25%, c'est une maison sans façade qui se développe depuis le niveau de la rue vers le bas. La Casa Guthrie n'est pas qu'une réponse au problème que pose un site en pente moyenne, mais une réflexion sur l'objectif final du système immobilier, c'est-à-dire vendre des maisons attractives à un bon prix.

CHILE

ASSADI & PULIDO ARCHITECTS

Project City Santiago
Typology Living
Completion Year 2007
Photos Assadi & Pulido Architects

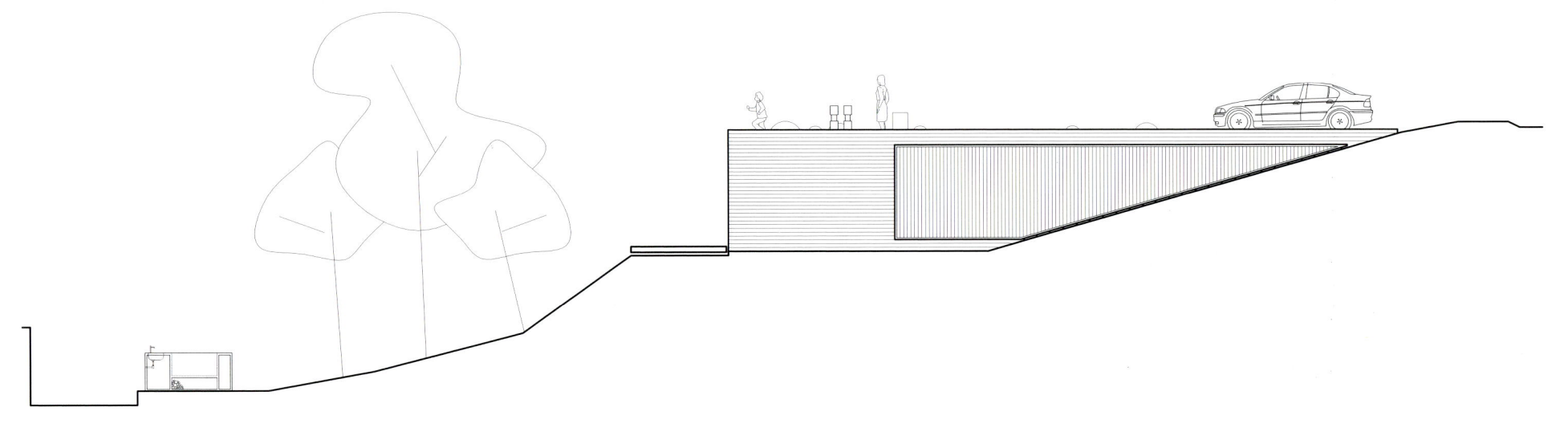

03

04

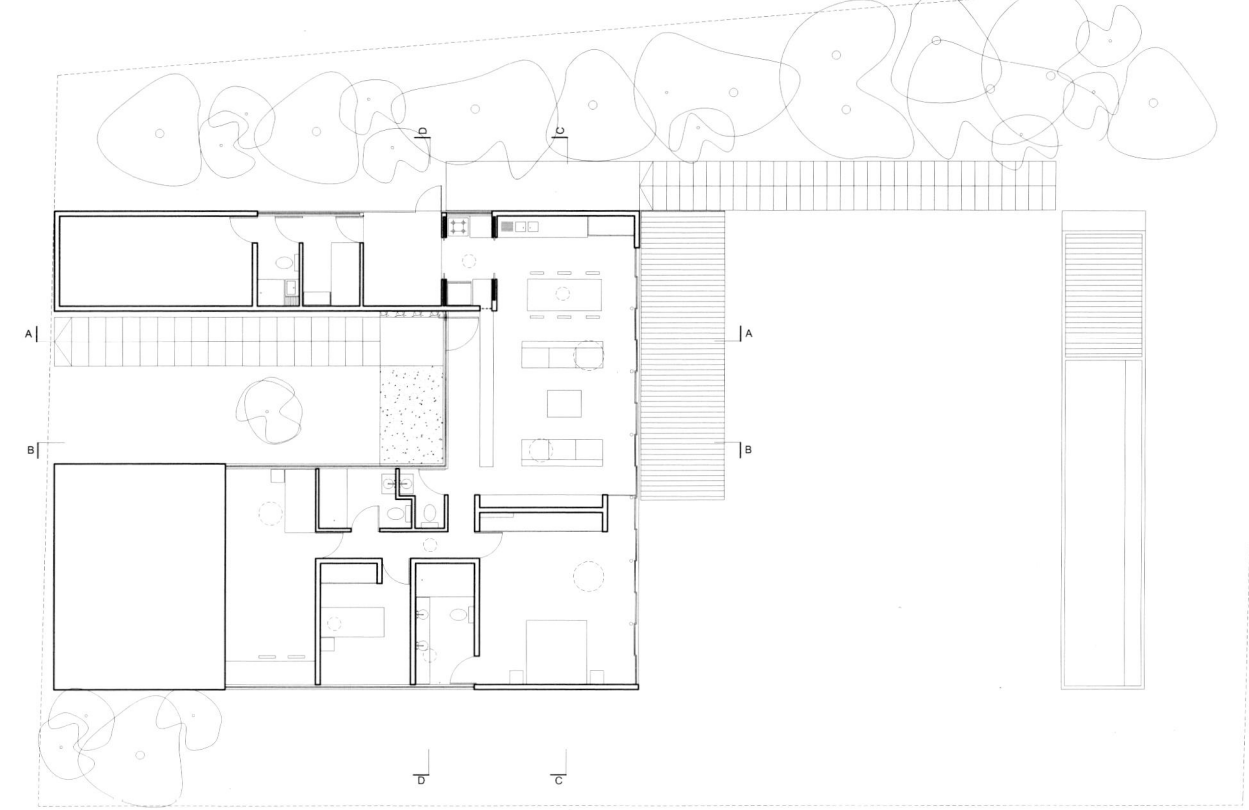

05

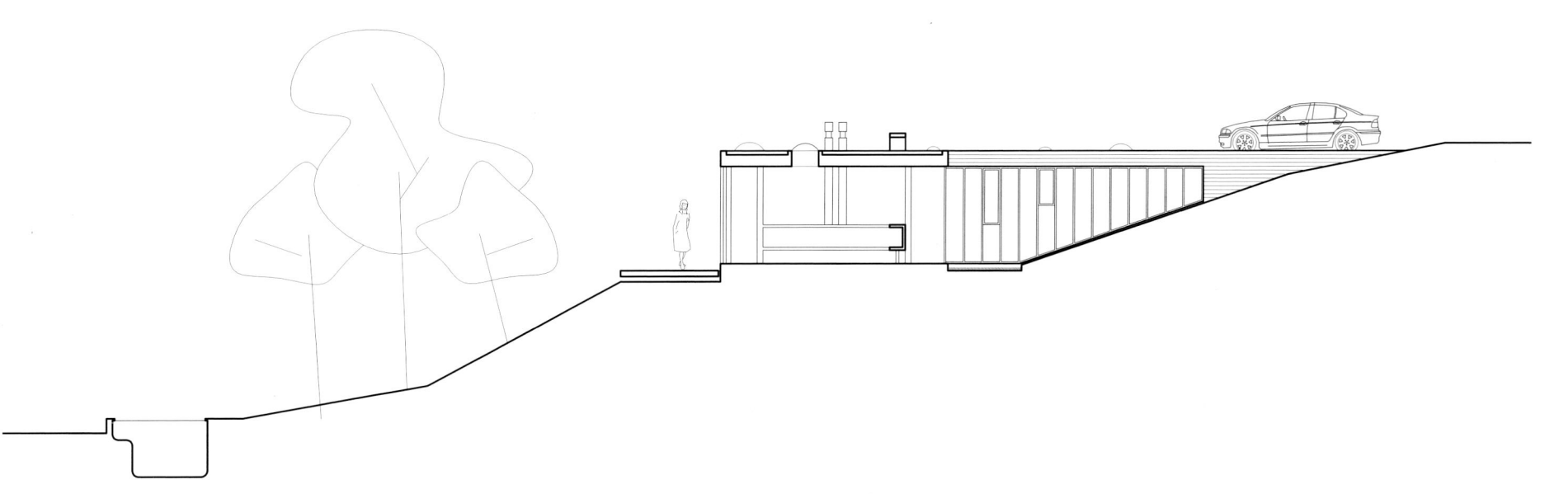

06

WALL HOUSE

01

01 Window detail

CHILE

FAR FROHN & ROJAS

E   **This project is** a design investigation into how the qualitative aspects of the wall, as a complex membrane, structure our social interactions and climatic relationships, enabling specific ecologies to develop. It breaks down the "traditional" walls of a house into a series of four delaminated layers (concrete cave, stacked shelving, milky shell, soft skin) in between which the different spaces of the house slip. Each layer is characterized by specific climatic, atmospheric, structural, material and functional properties.

ES   **Este proyecto es** una investigación de diseño en como los aspectos cualitativos de paredes, como una membrana compleja puede cambiar nuestras interacciones sociales y relaciones climáticas, permitiendo a ecologías específicas desarrollarse dentro del espacio. Rompe con las paredes "tradicionales" de una vivienda en una serie de cuatro capas separadas (un núcleo introvertido, repisas apiladas, una piel translucida y una membrana suave) entre los diferentes espacios que forman la casa. Cada capa se caracteriza a través de propiedades climáticas, atmosféricas, estructurales, materiales y funcionales.

D   **Das Projekt ist** eine ökologisch orientierte Designstudie darüber, wie die qualitativen Aspekte der Wand als eine komplexe Membran unsere sozialen Interaktionen und unser Verhältnis zum Klima mitbestimmen. Es löst die „traditionellen" Hauswände in eine Folge von vier geschichteten Lagen auf, zwischen denen die verschiedenen Räume des Hauses quasi hindurchschlüpfen. Jede dieser Schichten ist durch spezifische Eigenschaften hinsichtlich Klima, Atmosphäre, Struktur, Material und Funktion gekennzeichnet.

F   **Ce projet est** une enquête sur la manière dont les aspects qualitatifs du mur, comme une membrane complexe, structurent nos interactions sociales et nos relations climatiques, permettant le développement de technologies spécifiques. Il casse les murs « traditionnels » d'une maison en une série de quatre strates (cave en béton, étages enterrés, coque laiteuse, revêtement doux) au milieu desquelles glissent les différents espaces de la maison. Chaque strate est caractérisée par des propriétés climatiques, atmosphériques, structurelles, matérielles et fonctionnelles spécifiques.

Project City Santiago
Typology Living
Completion Year 2007
Photos Cristobal Palma

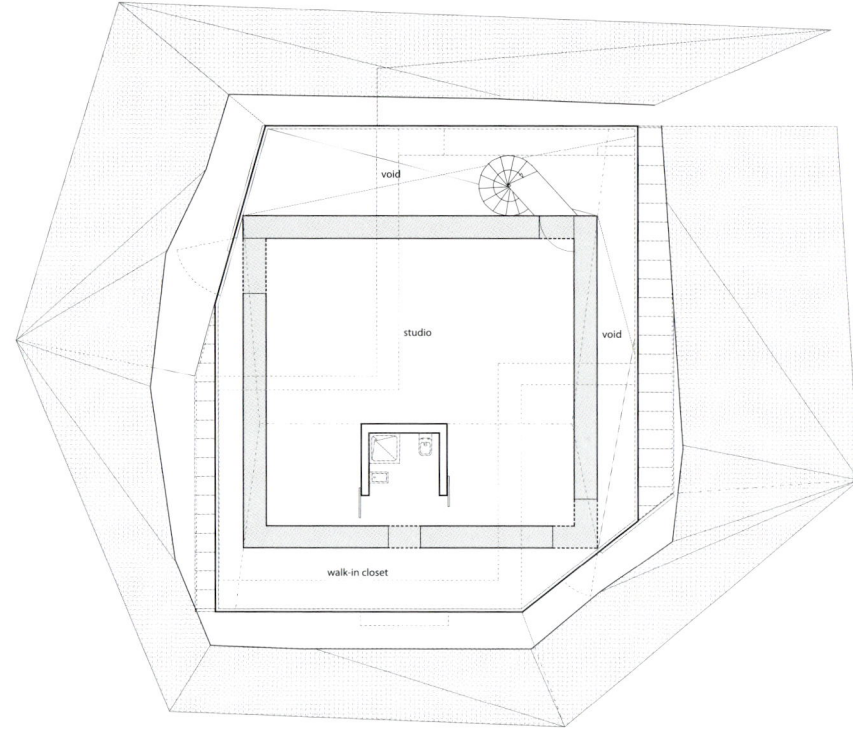

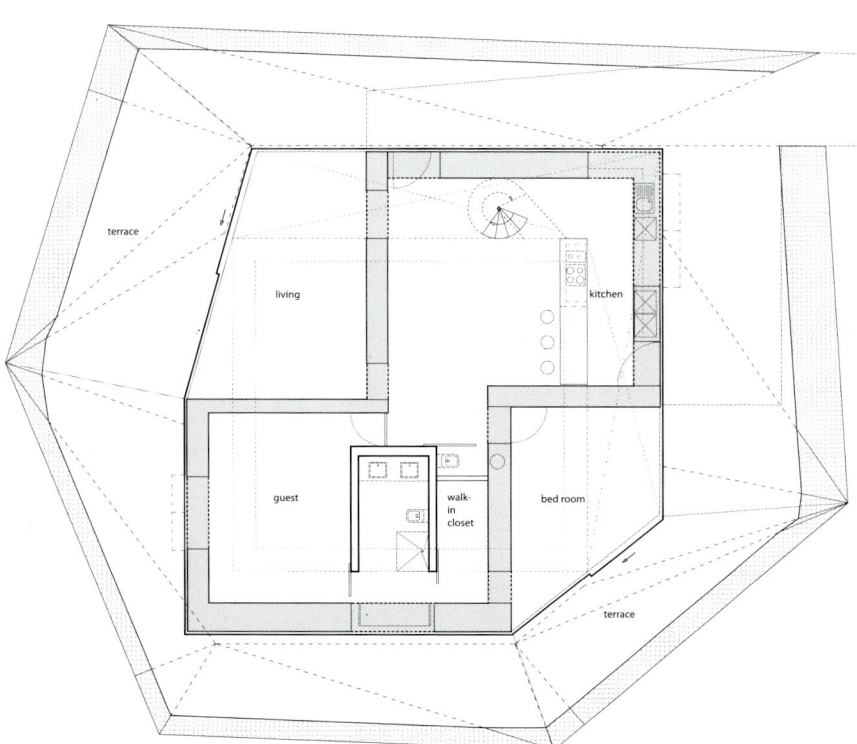

03

04

06   Rear view
07   Living room with sliding glass doors

CONTADOR-WELLER HOUSE

E   **The Contador-Weller** House, a weekend retreat in Valparaiso, was built using a Canadian timber fabrication system of prefab panels. The architects broke down the system and used the elements in different ways, panels as both structure and internal wall, with the modular units creating the basic grid for simplicity. This generated a total expression of the house, very distant from the classic Canadian model, but using the same system that was known by the builders.

ES   **La Casa Contador**-Weller, es una casa de fin de semana en Valparaíso, fue construida usando un sistema de fabricación de madera canadiense de paneles prefabricados. Los arquitectos rompieron con el sistema y usaron los elementos de formas diferentes, paneles tanto como estructura y como paredes internas, con las unidades modulares formando la rejilla básica para la simplicidad. Esto generó una expresión total de la casa, muy distante del modelo clásico canadiense, pero utilizando el mismo sistema conocido por los albañiles.

D   **Das Wochenendhaus wurde** unter Verwendung eines kanadischen Holz-Fertigungs-Systems aus vorgefertigten Platten errichtet. Die Architekten verwendeten zwar das System, nutzten die Elemente aber auf ganz andere Weise: Platten sind sowohl Konstruktionsstruktur wie auch Innenwand, mit den Moduleinheiten im Baukastenprinzip als Grundraster. Dies erlaubte ein ganz anderes Erscheinungsbild von dem Haus zu erzeugen, weit entfernt vom klassischen kanadischen Modell, aber unter Verwendung desselben Systems.

F   **La Contador-Weller** House, un refuge pour le weekend situé à Valparaiso, a été construite en utilisant un système de fabrication canadien en panneaux préfabriqués de bois. Les architectes ont cassé le système et utilisé les éléments de différentes manières : les panneaux comme murs de structure et cloisons, et les unités modulaires créant la base pour plus de simplicité. « Cela nous a permis de générer une expression totale de la maison », dit Riesco, « très loin du modèle canadien classique, mais en utilisant ce même système connu des constructeurs. »

01

01   View from deck to surrounding landscape

CHILE

RIESCO + RIVERA ARQUITECTOS ASOCIADOS CONTADOR

Project City Tunquen, Casablanca
Typology Living
Completion Year 2005
Photos Carlos Eguiguren

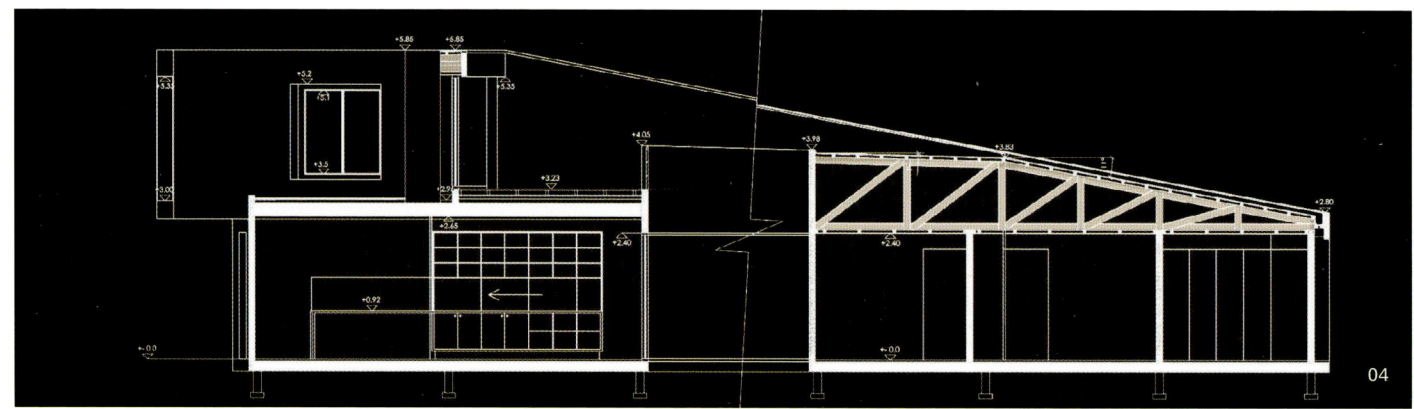

03   South elevation
04   Longitudinal section

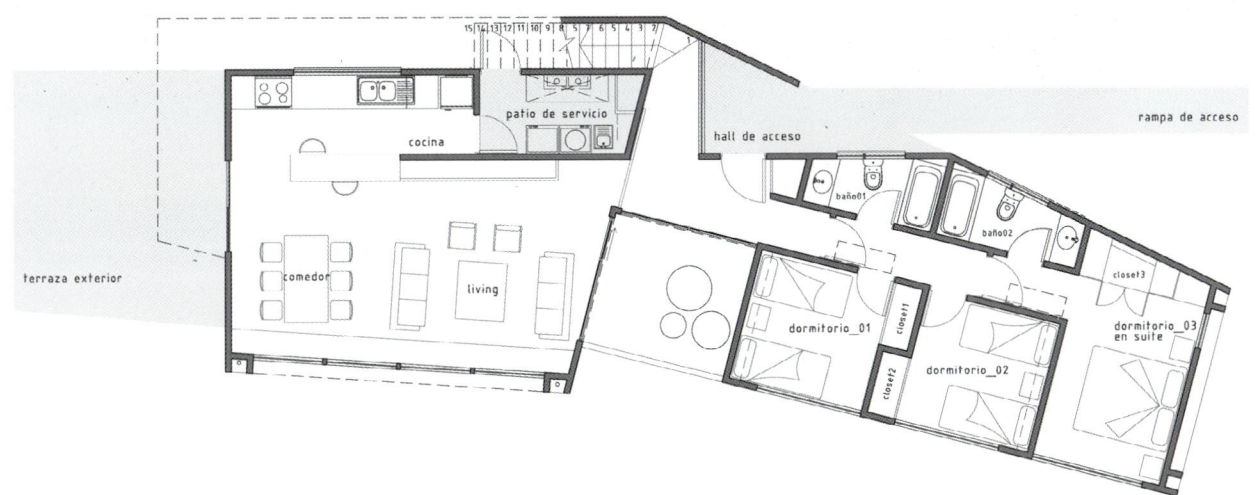

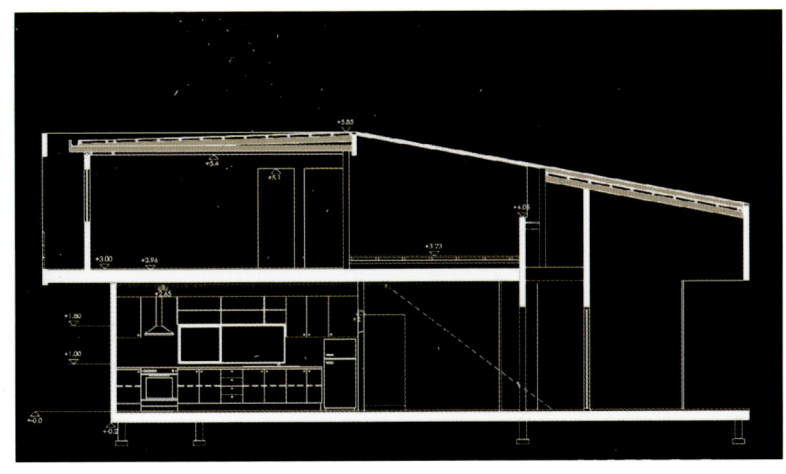

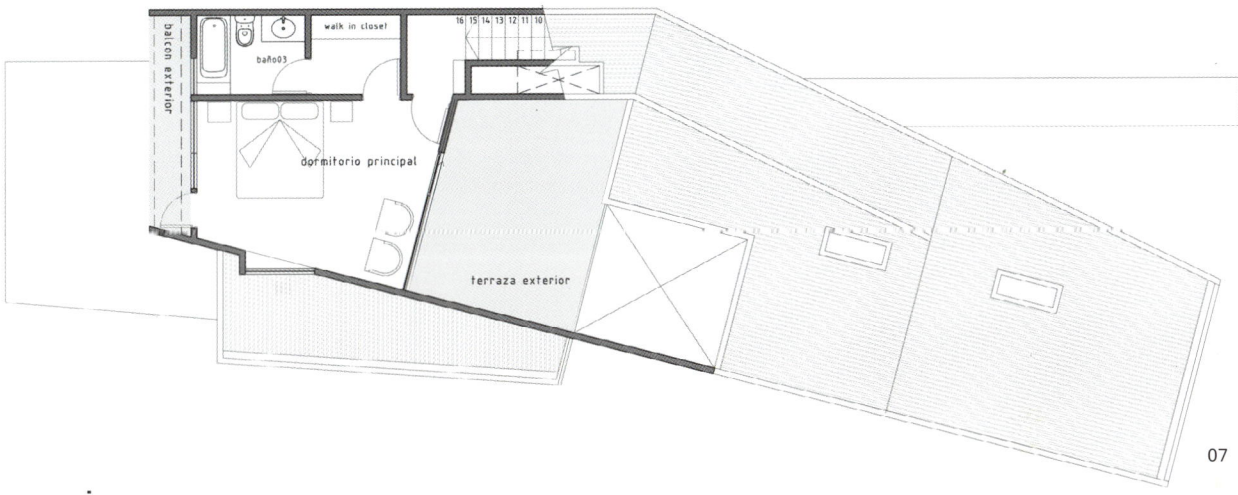

05

07

06

05 Cross-section
06 Detail façade
07 Second and first floor plan

39

KING ABDULAZIZ CENTER FOR KNOWLEDGE AND CULTURE

01

01 Building in context

E **The King Abdulaziz** Center for Knowledge and Culture is a bold new initiative on the Saudi Aramco Oil Company to promote cultural development within the Kingdom. The concept is both introverted and extroverted. Below grade the museum and archive functions are grouped around the inner void looking inwards to the truths and knowledge to be found within Saudi Aramco and the Kingdom of Saudi Arabia. Above grade, the composition reaches out of the ground, connecting to the world beyond.

ES **El Centro de** Rey Abdulaziz para el Conocimiento y la Cultura es una nueva iniciativa valiente sobre la Compañía petrolera saudita Aramco para promover el desarrollo cultural dentro del Reino. El concepto es tanto introvertido como extravertido. En el nivel inferior el museo y funciones de archivos son agrupados alrededor del vacío interior orientado hacia adentro a las verdades y el conocimiento dentro de Aramco saudita y el Reino de Arabia Saudita. En el nivel superior, la composición se extiende hacia el emplazamiento, uniéndose al mundo más allá.

D **Das König Abdulaziz** Zentrum für Wissen und Kultur ist eine Initiative der Saudi Aramco Ölgesellschaft, die kulturellen Entwicklungen innerhalb des Königreichs zu fördern. Der Entwurf gestaltet sich sowohl introvertiert als auch extrovertiert. Im Untergeschoss gruppieren sich Museums- und Archivfunktionen um einen inneren Leerraum. Nach innen richtet sich der Blick auf Wahrheiten und Wissen Saudi Aramcos und des Königreichs Saudi-Arabien. Im Obergeschoss erhebt sich die Anlage und tritt mit der jenseits liegenden Welt in Verbindung.

F **Le Roi Abdulaziz** Center pour la connaissance et la culture est une nouvelle initiative coutageuse du Saudi Aramco Oil Company pour favoriser le développement culturel dans le royaume. Le concept est introverti et extroverted. Au-dessous de la catégorie les fonctions de musée et d'archives sont groupées autour du vide intérieur regardant vers l'intérieur aux vérités et à la connaissance à trouver dans Aramco de Saoudien et le royaume de l'Arabie Saoudite. Au-dessus de la catégorie, la composition atteint hors de la terre, se reliant au monde là-bas.

UNITED ARAB EMIRATES
SNØHETTA

Project City Dhahran
Typology Culture / Public
Completion Year 2011
Photos MIR

02 Interior courtyard

03

04

03 Overall exterior view
04 Plaza
05 Oasis

06

06 Sectional view of exhibition area and concert hall
07 Auditorium

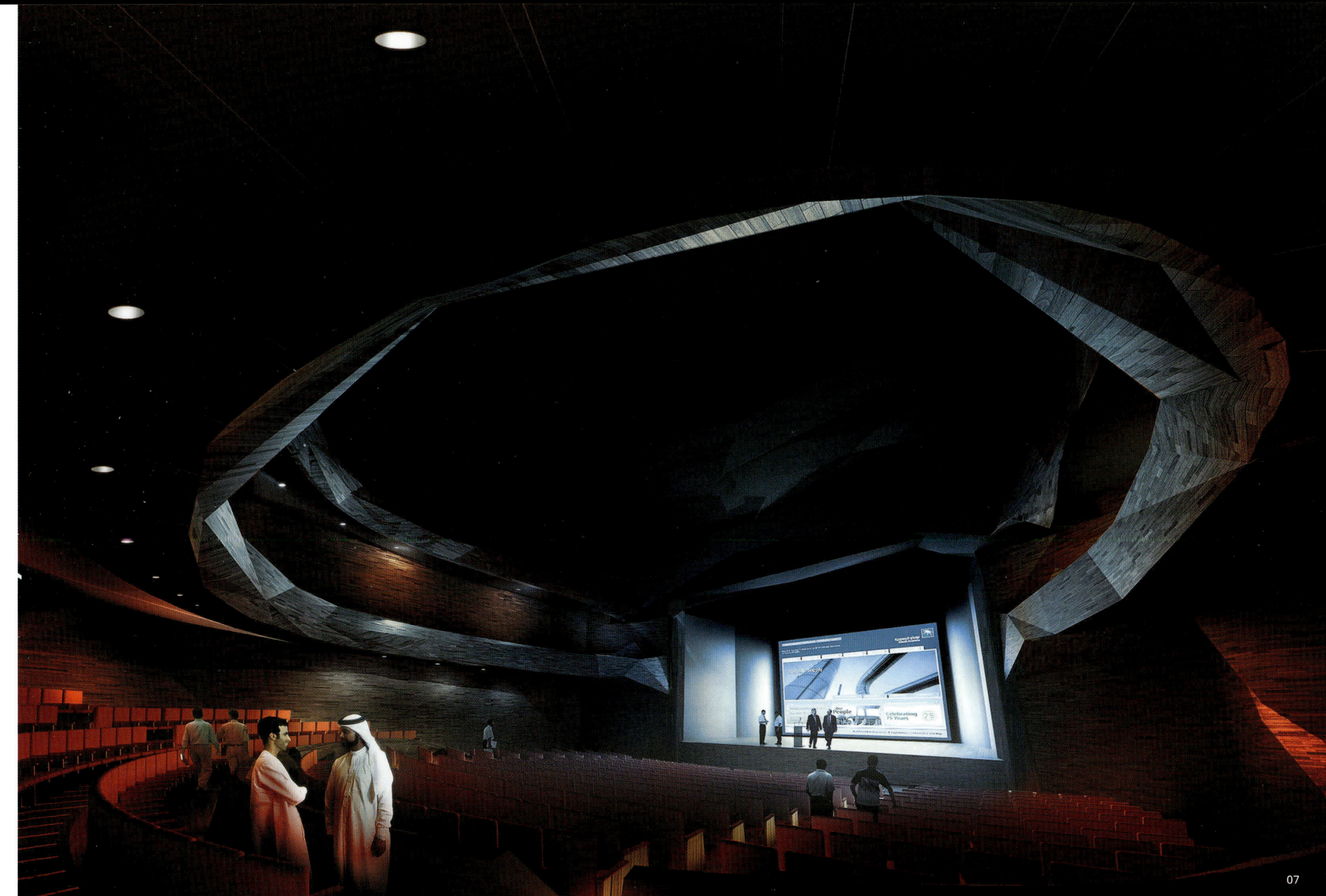

HELAL "NEW MOOON" RESIDENCE

01

01   Exterior view of canopy forming crescent moon

UNITED ARAB EMIRATES

STEVEN EHRLICH ARCHITECTS

GODWIN AUSTEN JOHNSON (EXECUTIVE ARCHITECT)

E   **Islamic culture is** embodied and reinterpreted through modern technology and design in this 43,056 square feet residence. Sheathed in shimmering aluminum, a massive curved roof shelters and unites the compound. The canopy forms a crescent moon, the symbol of new life that tops the minarets of Islam. The structure suggests a giant Bedouin tent, with the football-field-sized roof, cantilevered 30 feet on each side, casting a giant swathe of shade. A mashrabiyya, the traditional lattice sunscreen, filters direct sun.

ES   **La cultura islámica** es incorporada y reinterpretada por la tecnología moderna y el diseño en esta residencia de 4.000 metros cuadrados. Envainado en el brillo del aluminio, una azotea masiva curveada abriga y une el complejo. El pabellón forma una luna creciente, el símbolo de una nueva vida que encabeza los minaretes de Islam. La estructura sugiere una carpa beduina gigantesca, con el tejado del tamaño de un campo de fútbol, que se extiende 9 metros sobre cada lado, dejando una sobra gigante. Un mashrabiyya, el entremado tradicional solar, filtra el sol directamente hacia el interior.

D   **Auf insgesamt 4.000** Quadratmeter wird islamische Kultur mit moderner Technik und zeitgenössischem Design neu interpretiert. Ein massives, gewölbtes Dach aus schimmerndem Aluminium schützt und eint gleichsam die Gesamtanlage. Die Überdachung bildet einen Halbmond, Symbol neuen Lebens, das das islamische Minarette in der Regel bekrönt. Der Bau lässt an ein Beduinenzelt denken, dessen fußballplatzgroßes Dach auf jeder Seite neun Meter auskragt und somit einen gewaltigen Schatten wirft. Eine Mashrabiyya, der traditionelle gitterartige Sonnenschutz, filtert das Sonnenlicht.

F   **La culture musulmane** est incarnée et réinterprétée dans l'architecture et la technologie modernes de cette résidence de 4000 mètres carrés. Le toit courbe massif en aluminium scintillant abrite et unifie le tout. Le sommet forme une lune ascendante, le symbole de la nouvelle vie, qui surmonte traditionnellement les minarets. La structure évoque une tente de Bédouins géante, avec un toit de la taille d'un terrain de football, surélevé de 9 mètre sur chaque côté, créant une immense zone d'ombre. Un mashrabiyya, un écran solaire traditionnel en treillis, filtre la lumière directe du soleil.

Project City Dubai
Typology Living
Completion Year 2006
Photos Erhard Pfeiffer

02 Entrance area

03

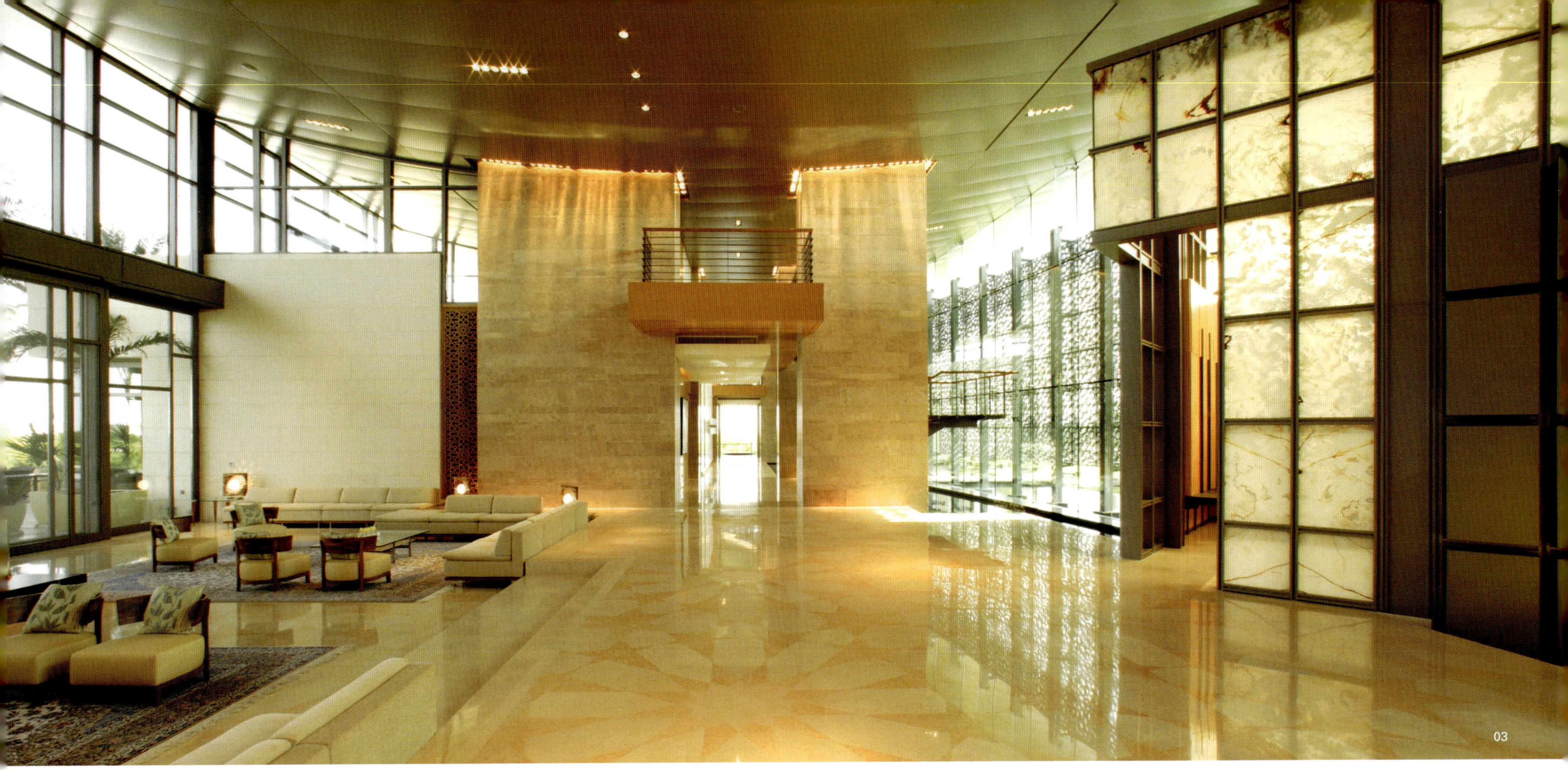

03 Interior view, lobby
04 East elevation
05 Interior view, detail mashrabiyya

04

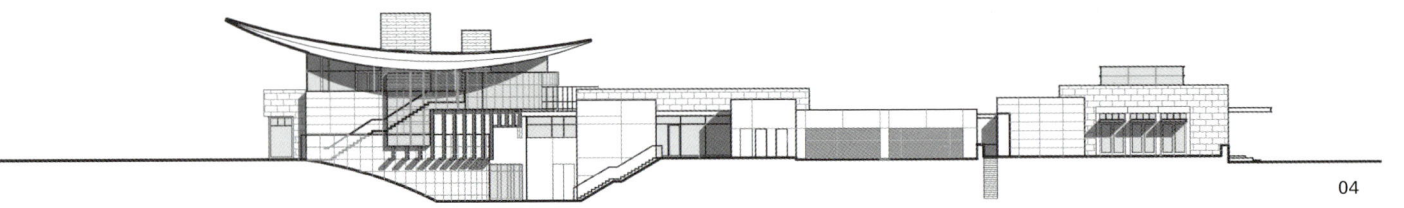

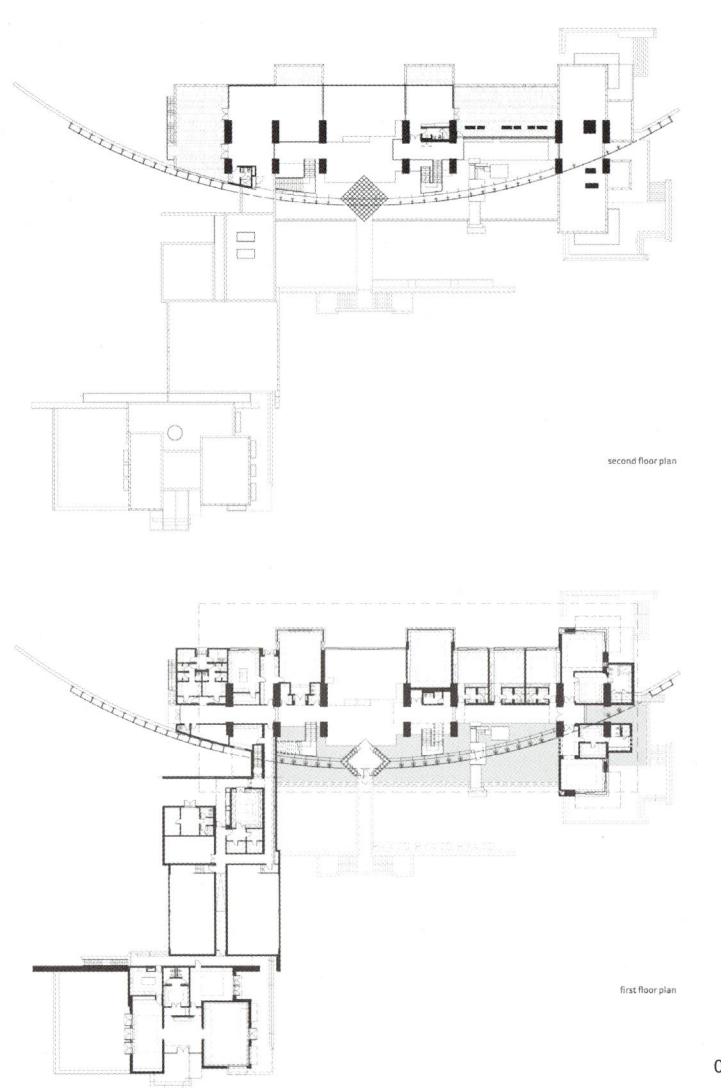

second floor plan

first floor plan

06

07

06   View to rear façade from pool area
07   Floor plans
08   Entry way

RAS AL-KHAIMAH-GATEWAY PROJECT

01

E   **Situated in the desert**, 93 miles east of Dubai in the emirate of Ras Al Khaimah, this project will mark the gateway to the emirate and form the entrance to the newly planned capital city. The architectural expression is inspired by the desert and mountain landscape, providing an infinite variety of naturally shaded, protected space, around which the multiple uses for development are woven. A 656 foot-high tower will be the setting for a five-star hotel affording panoramic views across the emirate and towards the gulf.

ES   **Situado en el** desierto del kilómetro 150, al Este de Dubai en el emirato de Ras Al Khaimah, este proyecto marcará la puerta al emirato y formará la entrada a la capital recién planificada. La expresión arquitectónica se inspira por el desierto y el paisaje montañoso, dotando una variedad infinita de espacios protegidos naturalmente, alrededor del cual se tejen múltiples empleos del desarrollo. Una torre de 200 metros de altura albergara un hotel de cinco estrellas ofreciendo vistas panorámicas a través del emirato y hacia el golfo.

D   **In der Wüste** gelegen, 150 Kilometer östlich von Dubai im Emirat Ras Al Khaimah, ist dieses Projekt als Wahrzeichen und Eingangstor für die neu geplante Hauptstadt des Emirats konzipiert. Der Entwurf ist maßgeblich durch die Wüsten- und Berglandschaft inspiriert, welche eine unendliche Vielfalt natürlich beschatteter, geschützter Bereiche bietet. Um diese werden die verschiedenen Funktionsbereiche entwickelt. Ein 200 Meter hoher Turm wird ein Fünf-Sterne-Hotel beherbergen, das einen Panorama-Ausblick über das Emirat bis hin zum Golf ermöglicht.

F   **Situé dans le** désert, à 150 kilomètre à l'est de Dubai, dans l'émirat de Ras Al Khaimah, ce projet marquera le passage vers l'émirat et formera l'entrée de la capitale dont la fondation a récemment été prévue. L'expression architecturale est inspirée par le paysage désertique et montagneux, offrant une variété infinie d'espaces naturellement ombragés et protégés, autour desquels les multiples développements possibles se tissent. Une tour de 200 mètres de haut abritera un hôtel cinq étoiles offrant une vue panoramique sur l'émirat et vers le golfe.

UNITED ARAB EMIRATES
SNØHETTA

Project City Ras Al-Khaimah
Typology Commercial
Completion Year in progress
Renderings MIR

02 Hotel's front façade

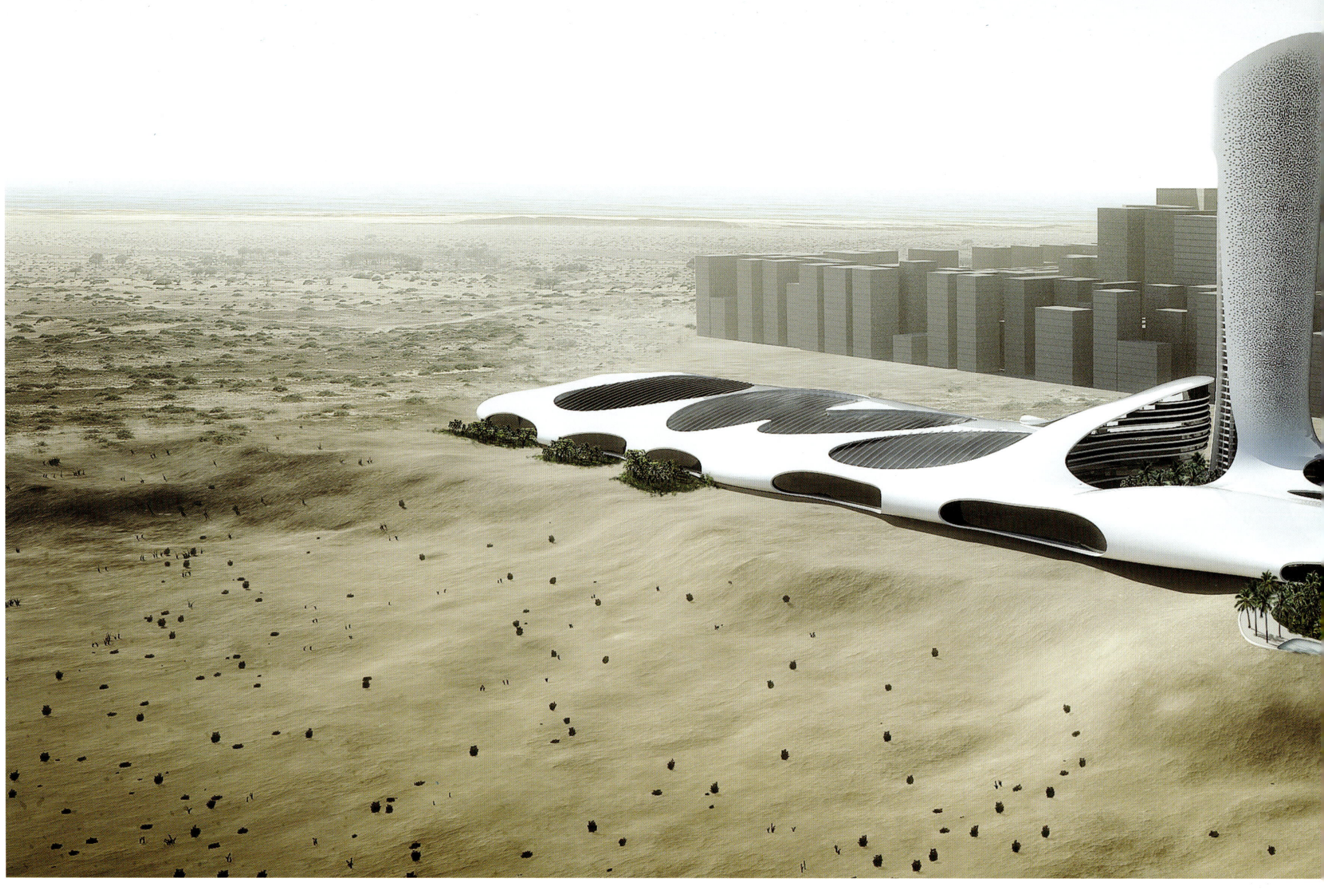

03 Gateway project's perspective

DESERT BROOM PUBLIC LIBRARY

01   Interior view

E   **Borrowing from the** symbiotic relationship of a young saguaro cacti and its nurse tree along the arroyos edge, the expansive roof of the library creates a shaded microclimate, providing filtered daylight, shelter, and a nurturing environment for intellectual growth and development. This project's strength is in the integration of the exterior with the interior of the building. The roof form extends above an adjoining arroyo 60 feet out into the natural desert, creating indoor and outdoor transitional spaces.

ES   **Tomando como punto** de partida la relación simbiótica de un cactus jóven saguaro y su árbol nutriente a lo largo del borde de los arroyos, el tejado de gran extensión de la biblioteca crea un microclima protegido del sol, proporcionando la luz del día filtrada, refugio, y un ambiente que nutre para el crecimiento intelectual y el desarrollo. La potencia de este proyecto está en la integración del exterior con el interior del edificio. La forma del tejado se extiende encima del arroyo adyacente 18 metros hacia fuera en el desierto natural, creando espacios de interior y exteriores de transición.

D   **An die symbiotische** Beziehung eines jungen Saguaro-Kaktus' und seines Wirtbaumes erinnernd, erzeugt das ausladende Dach der Bibliothek ein schattiges Mikroklima und liefert so den Nutzern gefiltertes Tageslicht, Schutz und eine dem Lesen und Lernen förderliche Umgebung. Die Stärke des Projekts liegt in der Integration des Gebäudeinneren mit dem Äußeren. Die Dachform dehnt sich über ein angrenzendes 18 Meter langes Flussbett bis in die Wüstenlandschaft hinein aus und schafft Übergänge zwischen Innen und Außen.

F   **Empruntant à la** relation symbiotique du jeune cactus saguaro et de son arbre abri, le vaste toit de la bibliothèque crée un microclimat ombragé le long des bordures d'arroyos, offrant une lumière du jour filtrée et un cadre enrichissant pour la croissance et le développement intellectuels. La force de ce projet est l'intégration de l'extérieur dans le bâtiment. La forme du toit s'étend sur 18 mètres au-dessus des arroyos, vers le désert naturel, créant un espace transitionnel entre intérieur et extérieur.

USA

RICHÄRD+BAUER

Project City Cave Creek (AZ)
Typology Public
Completion Year 2005
Photos Bill Timmerman Photography

03 Extended roof into desert
04 Deck
05 Floor plan

04

05

DESERT HOUSE

01

01 Total view

E   **The Desert House** employs four house-modules and six deck-modules, to suit the wide-open desert landscape. The desert climate inspired the architects to create covered outdoor living areas. By forming an "L," the home establishes a protected exterior environment that includes a pool and fire pit. The Desert House derives most of its power from solar panels, while sunshades on the south and west façades minimize the impact of harsh summer sun. In colder months, concrete floors provide passive solar heat gain.

ES   **Desert House (Casa** del Desierto) emplea cuatro módulos habitacionales y seis módulos de cubierta, para encajar en el extenso paisaje desértico. El clima del desierto inspiro a los arquitectos para crear zonas exteriores cubiertas. Con su forma de una " L ", la casa conforma un espacio exterior protegido que incluye una piscina y un pequeño foso para hacer fuego. La mayor parte de la energía la obtiene de paneles solares, mientras las fachadas cubiertas al sur y al oeste minimizan el impacto del tórrido sol estival. En los meses más fríos, el suelo de hormigón almacena el calor del sol.

D   **Das Desert House** besteht aus vier Haus- und sechs Terrassenmodulen, um sich der offenen Wüstenlandschaft anzupassen. Das Klima inspirierte die Planer, überdachte Außenwohnbereiche zu schaffen. Durch die L-Form des Hauses entsteht ein geschützter Außenbereich mit Pool und Feuerstelle. Das Gebäude erhält den größten Teil seiner Energie durch Sonnenkollektoren, während an den Süd- und West-Fassaden Sonnenblenden die extreme Sommersonne mindern. In kühlen Monaten geben die Betonböden passive Solarwärme ab.

F   **La Desert House** utilise quatre modules de maison et six modules de terrasse, pour s'accorder à l'immensité du paysage désertique. Le climat du désert a inspiré les architectes pour créer des espaces de vie extérieurs couverts. Avec sa forme en « L », la maison crée un environnement extérieur protégé comprend une piscine et un barbecue. La Desert House tire la majeure partie de son énergie de panneaux solaires, tandis que des parasols sur les façades sud et ouest réduisent l'impact du chaud soleil d'été. Pendant les mois les plus frais, les sols en béton permettent un gain de chaleur solaire passive.

USA
Marmol Radziner and Associates

Project City Desert Hot Springs (CA)
Typology Living
Completion Year 2006
Photos Benny Chan, Fotoworks

03 Interior view, living room
04 Detail pool
05 Interior view, kitchen space
06 Protected exterior space

07

07 View to pool from deck
08 Front façade

WATER + LIFE MUSEUMS

01

01   General view

E   **Water + Life** Museum Campus celebrates and commemorates the link between Southern California's water infrastructure and the evolution of life. The educational museums are designed as living examples of environmental sustainability and efficiency. It is the first museum to gain Platinum-LEED status. The modern design is in the tradition of monumental, honorific architecture, and features steel-clad monoliths blazing across each façade, while latticed loggias give a dramatic processional feeling through filtered light.

ES   **El Water +** Life Museum Campus celebra y conmemora el vínculo entre la infraestructura de agua del Sur de California y la evolución de vida. Los museos educativos estan diseñados como ejemplos vivos del mantenimiento ambiental y eficacia. Este es el primer museo que ha sido otorgado el estado Platino-LEED. El diseño moderno está en la tradición de arquitectura monumental, honorifica, y destaca monolitos blindados que brillan a través de cada fachada, mientras loggias enrejadas dan un sentimiento processional dramático por la luz filtrada.

D   **Mit diesem Projekt** wird der Zusammenhang zwischen der Wasserversorgungs-Infrastruktur Südkaliforniens und der Entwicklung des Lebens zelebriert. Die Museen sind wegweisende Beispiele für Nachhaltigkeit und Umwelteffizienz, wofür sie auch ausgezeichnet wurden (Platinum-LEED Status). Das zeitgenössische Design steht in einer Tradition ehrwürdiger monumentaler Architektur, bestehend aus stahlverkleideten funkelnden Monolithen, während gitterartige Kolonnadenbauten durch eindringendes gefiltertes Licht dramatische Effekte erzielen.

F   **Le Water + Life** Museum Campus célèbre le lien entre les infrastructures en eau de Californie du sud et l'évolution de la vie. Les musées éducatifs sont conçus comme des exemples vivants de développement durable et d'efficacité énergétique. C'est le premier musée à avoir obtenu le statut Platinum-LEED. Le design moderne suit la tradition monumentale et honorifique de l'architecture de musée, et comprend des monolithes couverts d'acier flamboyants en face de chaque façade, tandis que des loggias en treillis confèrent au tout une ambiance processionnelle spectaculaire grâce à la lumière filtrée.

USA

LEHRER ARCHITECTS + GANGI DESIGN + BUILD

Project City Hemet (CA)
Typology Culture
Completion Year 2006
Photos Benny Chan, Fotoworks (01, 03), Tom Lamb

03 Detail latticed loggias
04 Detail steel-clad monolith
05 Exterior view
06 View from the street
07 Site plan

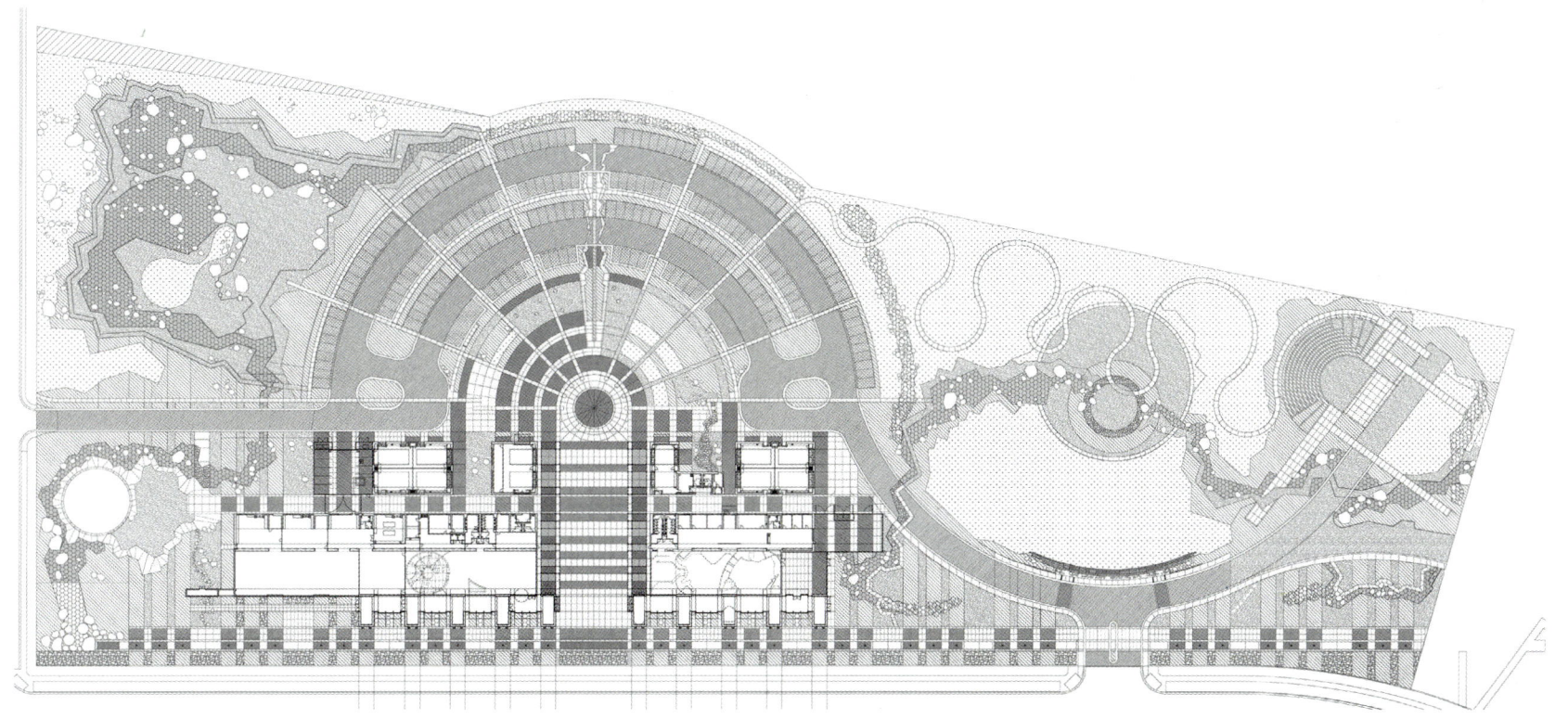

CESAR CHAVEZ LIBRARY

01

01 Exterior view by night

USA

Line & Spaces Architects, LLC Architects

E The 25,000-square-foot library is designed to serve a projected 40,000 visitors per month. Conceived as a "living room" for the expanding community, the library provides natural daylight, minimizing the use of conventional fixtures and offering occupants connection to the surrounding outdoors. Earth berms quietly integrate the library into the public parkscape, providing thermal mass against the building and a barrier from noise. Rainwater is harvested from the roof and stored in the adjacent lake for use in irrigation.

ES La biblioteca de 2.300 metros cuadrados fue diseñada para los 40.000 visitantes proyectados por mes. Concebida como "una sala de estar" para la amplia comunidad, la biblioteca proporciona la luz natural del día, reduciendo al mínimo el empleo de elementos convencionales y permitiendo una conexión con el exterior a los inquilinos. Las bermas de Tierra silenciosamente se integran a la biblioteca en el paisaje del parque público, proporcionando la masa termal contra el edificio y una barrera del ruido. El agua de lluvia se cosecha en los tejados y se almacena en el lago adyacente para el empleo en la irrigación.

D Die 2.300 Quadratmeter große Bibliothek wurde für etwa 40.000 Besucher monatlich angelegt. Als eine Art „Wohnzimmer" für die wachsende Gemeinde konzipiert, bietet sie natürliches Tageslicht und Verbindungen nach außen für die Nutzer. Böschungen integrieren die Bibliothek sanft in die öffentliche Parklandschaft, die unter anderem auch die Funktion als Lärmschutz gegenüber dem Gebäude haben. Regenwasser zur Bewässerung wird vom Dach gesammelt und im angrenzenden See gespeichert.

F La bibliothèque d'une surface de plus de 2300 mètres carrés est conçue pour accueillir les 40 000 visiteurs prévus chaque mois. Considérée comme une « salle de séjour » pour une communauté en pleine expansion, la bibliothèque offre une lumière du jour naturelle, réduisant l'utilisation de lustres conventionnels et offrant aux occupants un lien avec l'extérieur. Des bermes de terre intègrent tranquillement la bibliothèque dans le paysage public, procurant une masse thermique et une barrière contre le bruit. L'eau de pluie est collectée et stockée dans le lac adjacent pour l'irrigation.

Project City Laveen (AZ)
Typology Public
Completion Year 2007
Photos Bill Timmerman Photography

02   East elevation

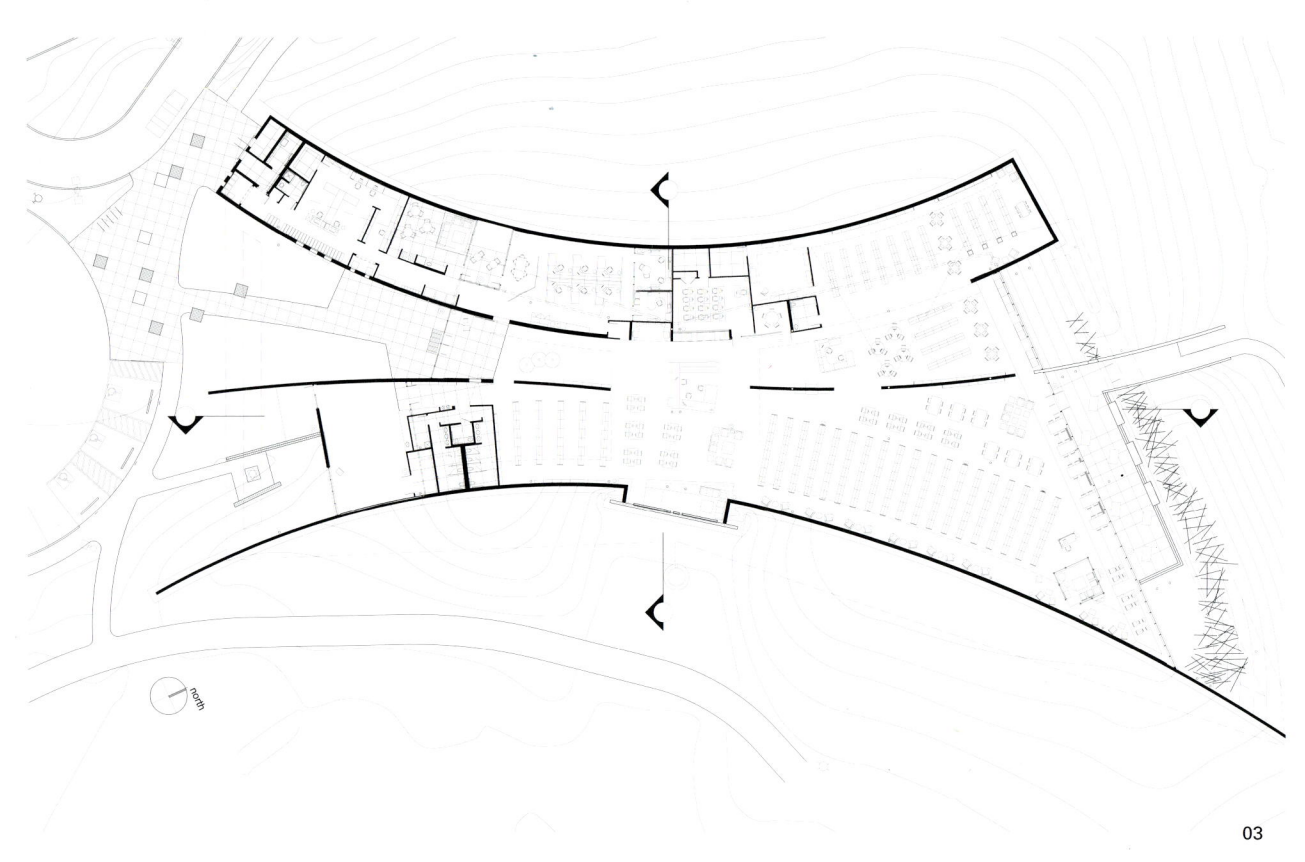

03

04

05

03 Floor plan
04 Entrance area
05 Light interior
06 Longitudinal section
07 North elevation

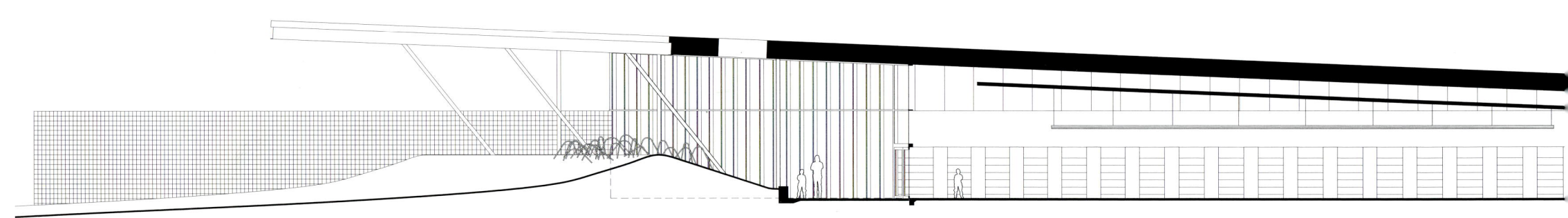

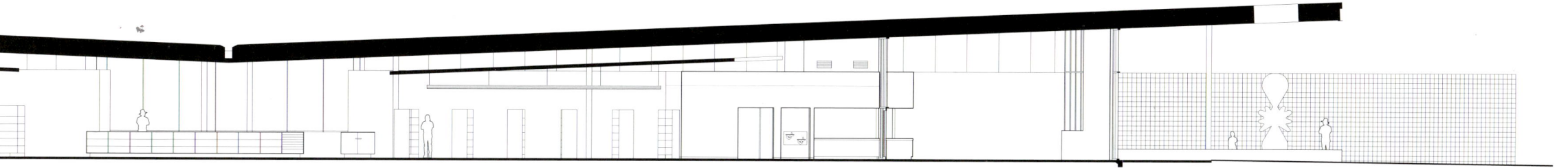

07

06

BROWN HOUSE

01

01 Detail staircase

E   **The country house**, situated in a partially wooded area with rolling hills was custom designed and built on site; the building's elements consist of panelization of walls, fabrication of custom hurricane clips, hybrid wood and steel wall structures, five different staircase designs, three custom window frames, doors, floors, and custom millwork. Green building techniques were integrated including passive solar, natural ventilation insulated concrete forms, R-45 roof insulation, radiant flooring, heat pumps, and a green roof system.

ES   **La casa de** campo, situada en un zona parcialmente boscosa con el terreno accidentado fue un encargo diseñada y construida en el emplazamiento; los elementos del edificio consisten en la panalización de paredes, fabricación de clips de huracán de encargo, estructuras para las paredes híbridas de madera y de acero, cinco diseños de escalera diferentes, tres marcos de ventana de encargo, puertas, pisos, y carpintería mecánica. Técnicas de edificio verdes fueron integradas incluyendo la ventilación pasiva solar, formas de hormingo para la ventilación natural aisladas, aislamiento de tejados R-45, el suelo radiante, bombas de calor, y un sistema de tejado verde.

D   **Das Landhaus liegt** in einem teils bewaldeten Gebiet mit sanft geschwungenen Hügeln. Alle Bauteile wurden maßgefertigt und vor Ort errichtet: die Wandtäfelung, spezielle Sturmverankerungen, hybride Stahl-Holz-Konstruktionen, fünf Treppenentwürfe sowie drei Fensterrahmen, Türen, Böden und sämtliche Holzarbeiten. Techniken des „Grünen Bauens" wurden integriert, diese umfassen passive Solarenergienutzung, natürliche Belüftung, R-45 Dach-Isolierung, Wärmepumpen und Dachbegrünung.

F   **Cette maison de** campagne, construite dans une zone de collines partiellement boisée, a été faite sur mesure et construite sur site. Les panneaux muraux, le système de fixation anti-ouragan, les structures murales hybrides en bois et acier, les cinq escaliers, les trois cadres de fenêtres, les sols, les portes et la menuiserie, tout a été conçu spécialement pour la maison. Des techniques de construction écologiques ont été intégrées, notamment le solaire passif, des formes en béton isolées avec ventilation naturelle, une isolation de toit R-45, le chauffage par le sol, des pompes à chaleur et un système de toit vert.

USA

RANDY BROWN ARCHITECTS

Project City Omaha (NE)
Typology Living
Completion Year in progress
Photos Farshid Assasi - Assassi Productions

03 Exterior view, detail panoramic window
04 Study room
05 Detail staircase
06 Floor plan
07 Floor-wall bed wooden surface

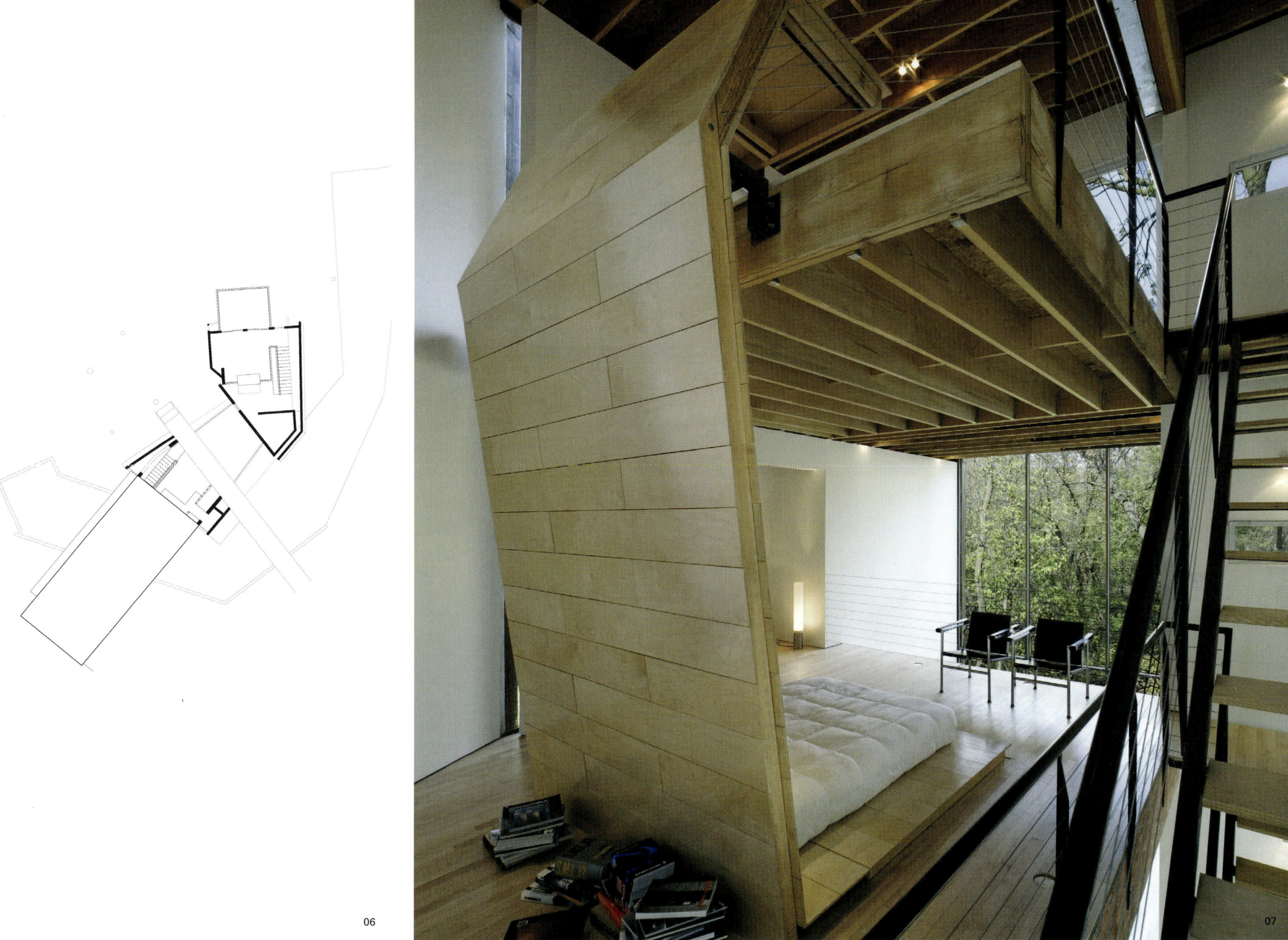

08

08 Wooden wall structure
09 Linking bridge
10 Detail staircase shaft

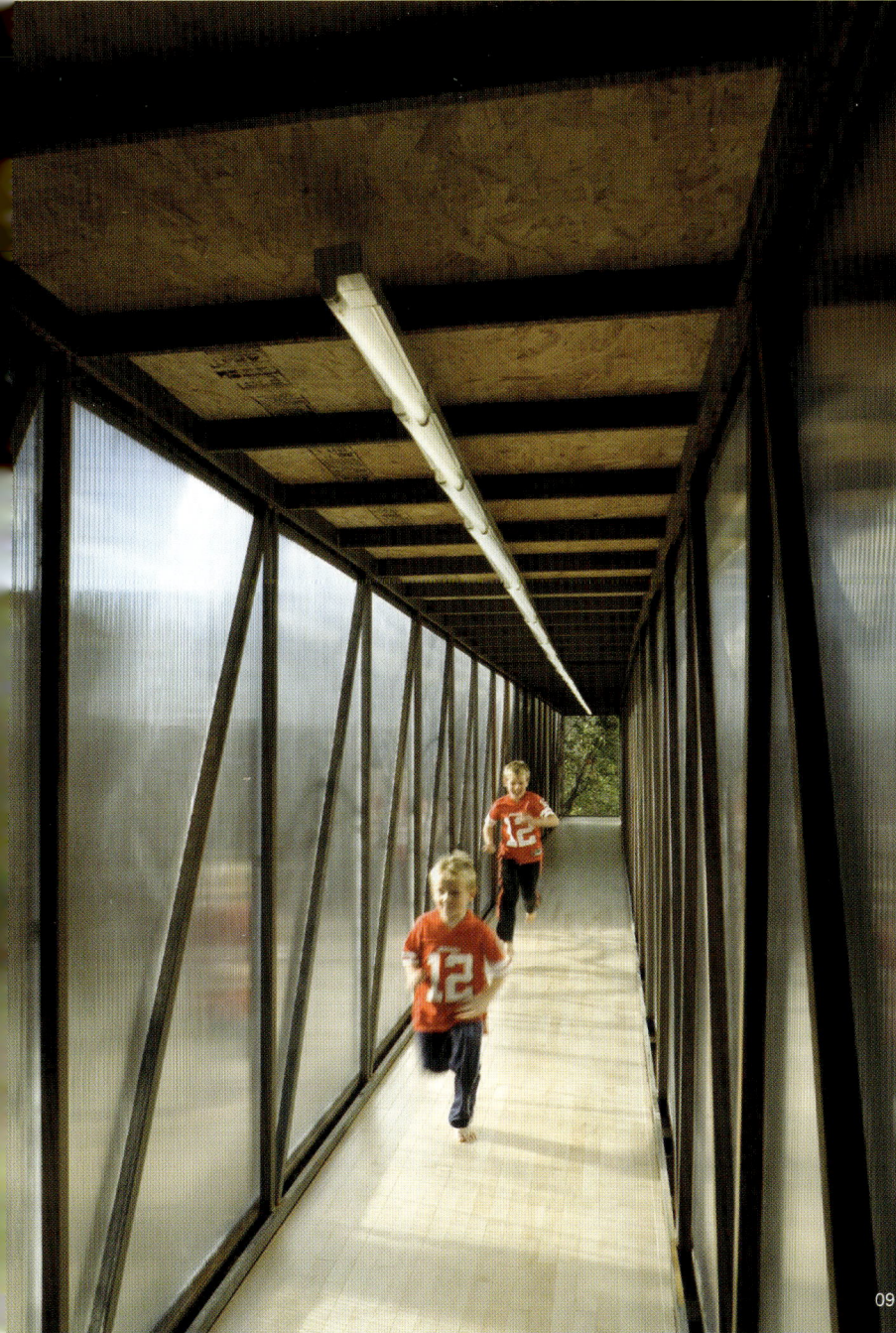

09

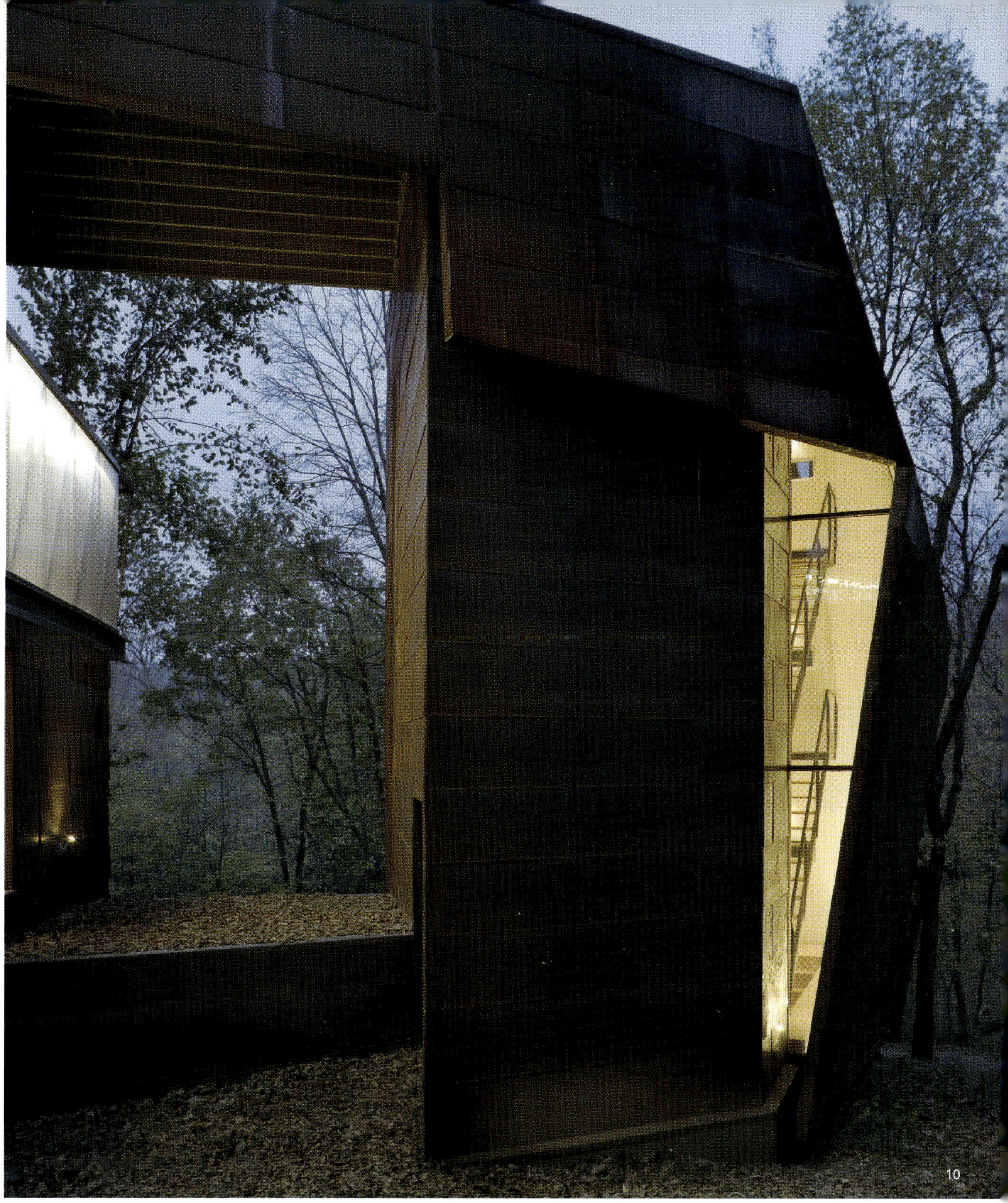
10

FRITZ RESIDENCE

E   **To achieve a** feeling of simplicity, the house reflects a strategy of enclosure and openness focused toward the main outdoor space. Two wings are connected together at the main living, dining, and kitchen space to define a corner with one wing containing the guest bedrooms and the other the master suite. Designed in the Modern idiom to reflect the Palm Springs location, the house is open, flowing, and bathed in natural light. All rooms access the outdoor pool/courtyard space through large sliding glass walls.

ES   **Para alcanzar la** simplicidad, la casa refleja una estrategia de recinto y apertura enfocada hacia el espacio principal del exterior. Dos alas se unen junto a los espacios principales: salon, comedor, y cocina para definir una esquina con una ala que aloja los dormitorios de invitados y el otro el dormitorio principal. Diseñado en un estilo Moderno para reflejar la ubicación de Palm Springs, la casa es amplia, flota y se baña en la luz natural. Todos los espacios tienen acceso a la piscina exterior y patio a traves de paredes de cristal grandes que se deslizan.

D   **Das Haus spiegelt** gleichzeitig Abgeschiedenheit und Offenheit gegenüber der umgebenden Landschaft wider. Zwei Flügel sind durch Wohn-, Ess- und Küchenbereich miteinander verbunden und definieren so eine Ecksituation: ein Flügel beherbergt den Gästebereich, der andere die Master-Suite. In seiner modernen Formensprache verweist das Design auf die Örtlichkeit Palm Springs. Es ist offen, fließend und in natürliches Licht getaucht, alle Räume führen durch große Schiebewände aus Glas nach außen zum Pool und Innenhof.

F   **Pour parvenir à** un sentiment de simplicité, une stratégie de fermeture et d'ouverture concentrée sur l'espace extérieur principal définit la maison. Les deux ailes sont reliées dans l'espace séjour, salle à manger, cuisine ; une aile contenant les chambres d'ami, et l'autre la suite parentale. Conçue dans un langage moderne pour refléter l'atmosphère de Palm Springs, la maison est ouverte, fluide et baignée de lumière naturelle. Toutes les chambres ont accès à l'espace cour/piscine extérieur, grâce à de grandes baies vitrées coulissantes.

01   Living room and access to outdoor space

USA
OJMR ARCHITECTS

Project City Palm Desert (CA)
Typology Living
Completion Year 2004
Photos Ciro Coelho

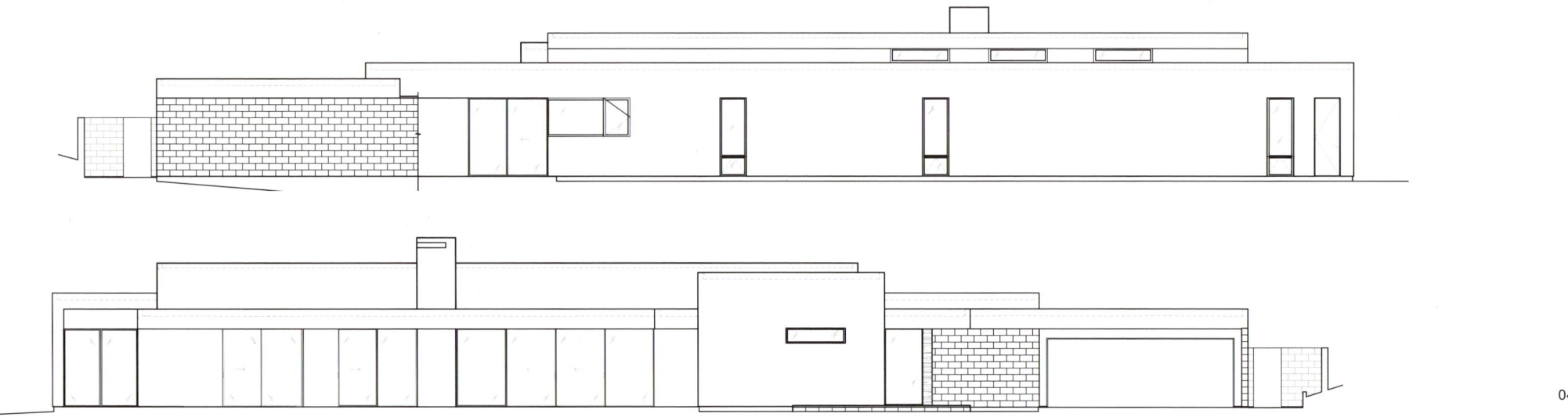

03

04

05

06

03 Exterior view by night from inner courtyard
04 Elevations
05 Entry way
06 Extended concrete roofs and pool area

2801 SOUTH PALM CANYON

E   **The 2801 South** Palm Canyon, residential development combines a Southern California Modernist style with a contemporary sensibility, providing a new model for high-quality desert home design, where the lines between indoor and outdoor spaces are blurred. The residential development includes 16 houses, all of which are new single-family homes in an area that is becoming increasingly urban.

ES   **El 2801 South** Palm Canyon, es un desarrollo residencial que combina un estilo de Modernista del Sur de California con una sensibilidad contemporánea, brindando un nuevo modelo del diseño de casas de alta calidad para el desierto, donde las divisiones entre espacios al aire libre y el interior desaparecen. El desarrollo residencial incluye 16 casas, todas unifamiliares en una zona que resulta cada vez más urbana.

D   **Das Bauprojekt verbindet** südkalifonisch-modernistischen Stil mit zeitgenössischer Sensibilität und schafft so eine Form hochwertiger Gestaltung von Wüstenarchitektur, bei der die Grenzen zwischen Innen- und Außenräumen verwischen. In einer sich zunehmend verstädternden Gegend umfasst diese innovative und moderne Wohnanlage 16 neue Einfamilienhäuser.

F   **Le projet du** 2801 South Palm Canyon a été conçu et coélaboré par OJMR Architects, et marie un style moderniste du sud de la Californie avec une sensibilité contemporaine, offrant un nouveau modèle de maison du désert de grande qualité. Dans une zone qui devient de plus en plus urbaine, cette extension résidentielle novatrice et moderne comprend 16 maisons familiales individuelles. Créant dans un style qu'on appelle « moderne nouveau siècle », Reynolds efface les frontières entre les espaces intérieurs et extérieurs.

01   Exterior view form the street

USA

OJMR ARCHITECTS

Project City Palm Springs (CA)
Typology Living
Completion Year 2007
Photos Erhard Pfeiffer, Clark Dugger (03, 05)

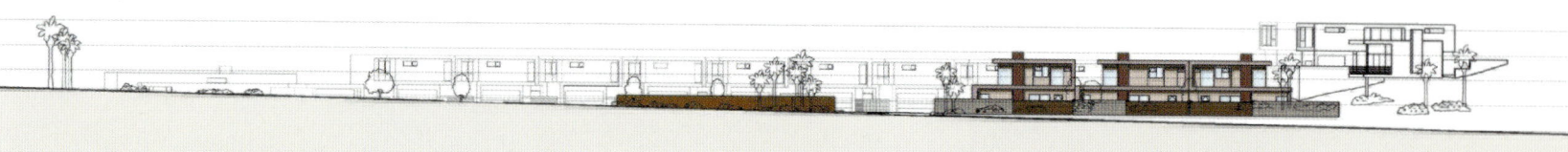

03

04

03 Deck and pool
04 Elevation
05 Single-family homes, entrances facing the street
06 Interior view
07 View into outdoor area

05

06

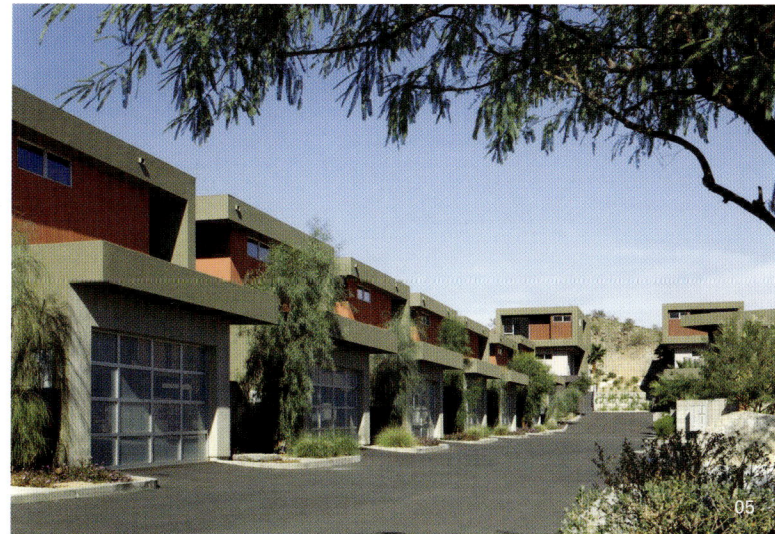

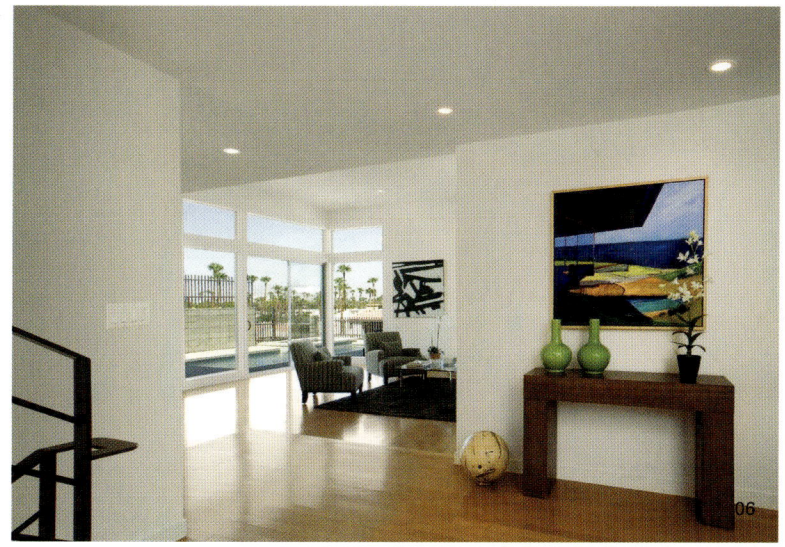

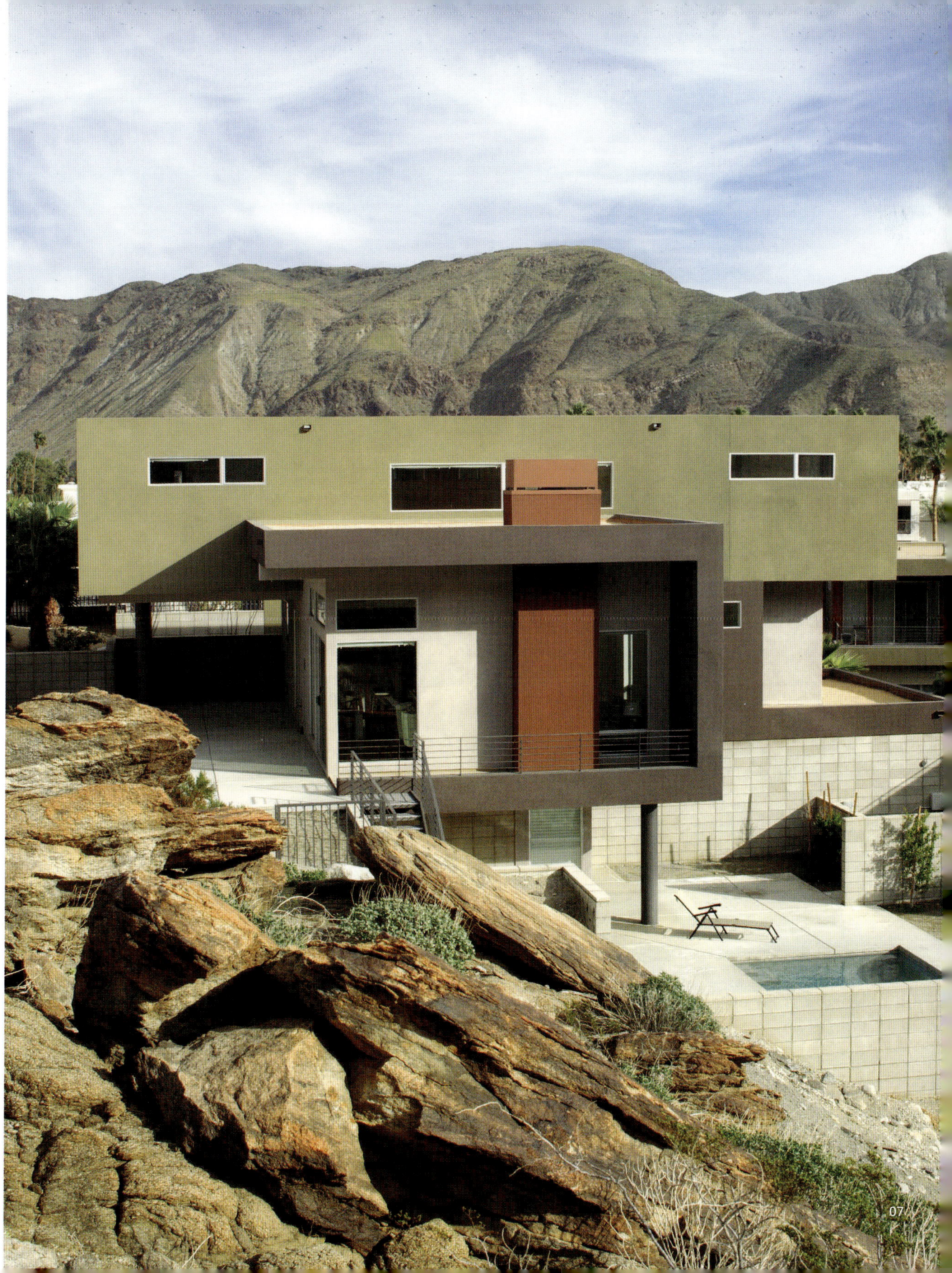

07

ALTA, PALM SPRINGS

01 Interior view, great room

E   **The butterfly roof**, an asymmetrical cantilever, reinforces the sense of orientation, opening maximum views to the mountains and sky. From the outside, the roof appears to float over the house, giving it a character of an outdoor/indoor pavilion. The great room, kitchen and dining room open out to the front courtyard as well as to the back, which has Zen-type quiet outdoor settings. The courtyard serves as a centerpiece of the house, with the sinuous lines of the pool serving as an invitation to experience the space.

ES   **El tejado de** forma de mariposa, un voladizo asimétrico, refuerza el sentido de orientación de la casa, abriendo vistas máximas a las montañas y el cielo. Del exterior, el tejado aparece flotar sobre la casa, dándole un carácter de un pabellón de exterior e interior. El salon, la cocina y el comedor se abren al patio delantero así como a la parte trasera, con un patio tranquilo tipo Zen. El patio sirve como un espacio central de la casa, con las líneas sinuosas de la piscina que sirve como una invitación para experimentar el espacio.

D   **Das Flügeldach betont** als asymmetrische Auskragung die Ausrichtung des Gebäudes und eröffnet den weitest möglichen Ausblick auf Berge und Himmel. Von außen scheint das Dach über dem Gebäude zu schweben und gibt ihm so den Charakter eines Außen-Innen-Pavillons. Der Hauptraum, Küche und Speisezimmer öffnen sich zum vorderen Innenhof ebenso wie zur Rückwand, hinter der sich eine ruhige zen-inspirierte Außenanlage anschließt. Der Innenhof ist das Herzstück des Projekts; hier schafft die geschmeidige Linie des Pools eine ganz eigene Raumerfahrung.

F   **Le toit papillon**, un porte-à-faux asymétrique, renforce l'axe d'orientation, ouvrant la vue la plus dégagée possible sur les montagnes et le ciel. Depuis l'extérieur, le toit semble flotter au-dessus de la maison, lui donnant l'aspect d'un pavillon intérieur/extérieur. La grande pièce, cuisine et salle à manger, s'ouvre sur la cour de devant ainsi qu'à l'arrière, dont l'extérieur est serein, d'un style zen. La cour intérieure sert de cœur au projet, les lignes sinueuses de la piscine constituant une invitation à découvrir l'espace.

USA
PATEL ARCHITECTS

Project City Palm Springs (CA)
Typology Living
Completion Year 2007
Photos Arthur Coleman

03 Entrance area

04

05

XEROS RESIDENCE

01

01 North elevation

E **Located within a** 1950's era development, the Xeros Residence creates a dramatic presence. The live-work design accommodates a design studio on the lower level and a single-story residence on the upper level accessible only by an external stair. The primary building material is exposed steel that weathers naturally and meld with the color of the surrounding hills. The residence is dubbed 'Xeros' to serve as a reminder that all design solutions should be in direct response to the environment.

ES **Situada dentro de** un desarrollo de los años 50, Xeros Residence crea una presencia dramática. El espacio de vivienda y trabajo (live/work) aloja un estudio de diseño sobre el nivel inferior y una vivienda de un nivel en la parte superior, sólo accesible por una escalera externa. Los materiales de construcción primarios son el acero expuesto que con el tiempo se desgasta naturalmente y funde con el color de las colinas circundantes. La residencia se apoda 'Xeros' para servir como un recordatorio de que todas las soluciones de diseño deberían responder directamente al ambiente.

D **Umgeben von 50er** Jahre Bebauung schafft der Baukörper eine dramatische Präsenz. Die Bereiche Wohnen und Arbeiten kombinierend, beherbergt er im unteren Geschoss ein Atelier, im oberen eine einstöckige Wohnung, die nur durch eine externe Treppe zugänglich ist. Das Hauptbaumaterial ist Sichtstahl, der natürlich verwittert und so mit der Farbe der umgebenden Hügel eins wird. Der Name des Objekts „Xeros" verweist auf die Idee, dass alle Entwurfslösungen im Einklang mit der Umwelt stehen sollten.

F **Située dans une** zone de développement des années 50, la résidence Xeros a une présence spectaculaire. Son architecture vie/travail abrite un atelier de design au niveau inférieur et une résidence sur un seul niveau au premier étage, accessible uniquement par un escalier extérieur. La matière première du bâtiment est l'acier apparent qui vieillit naturellement et se fond dans la couleur des collines environnantes. La résidence a été nommée « Xeros » (de la terre) pour rappeler que toutes les solutions de design doivent être une réponse directe à l'environnement.

USA
BLANK STUDIO

Project City Phoenix (AZ)
Typology Living
Completion Year 2006
Photos Bill Timmerman Photography

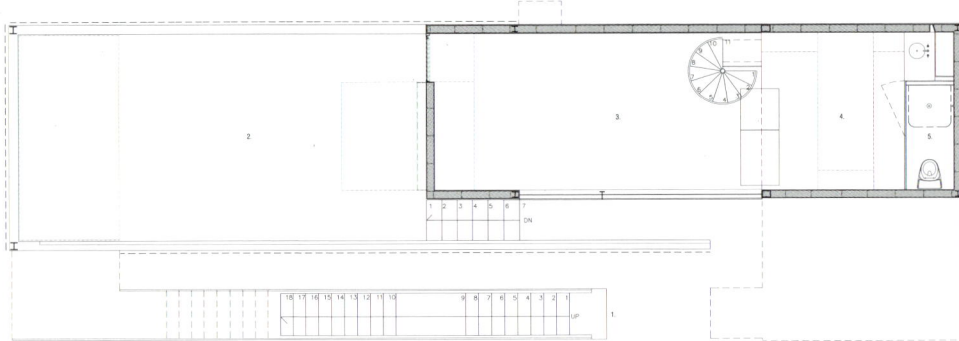

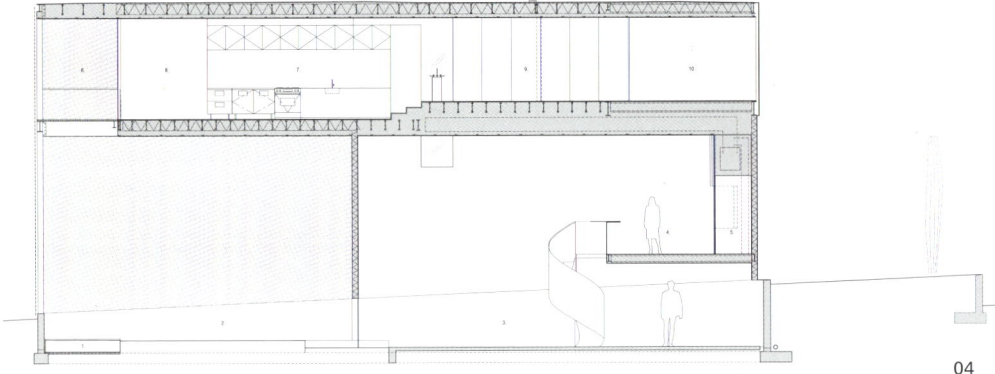

03

04

03 Exterior view
04 Floor plan and section
05 Detail external stair to upper level

06 Interior view, open kitchen area

07 Interior view, studio below
08 Exterior courtyard below

MARIPOSA RESIDENCE

01

01 Detail meditation chapel wrapped in channel glass

USA

DE BARTOLO ARCHITECTS

E **Commissioned by the** Brophy Jesuit Community to design a new home for ten Jesuit Priests, the scheme draws inspiration from the two existing white-flowering oleander hedges. The program for the residence called for a public zone of the house including the kitchen, living room, study, library, chapel, and a private zone, including the ten individual dwellings. Based on simple principles of light, shade and orientation, the house is shaped by climate and function where many of the spaces have a singular relationship to light.

ES **Comisionado por la** Comunidad Brophy jesuita para diseñar una nueva casa para diez Sacerdotes jesuitas, el esquema dibuja la inspiración de los dos setos de adelfa existentes de flores blancas. La casa consiste en una zona pública que se consiste de la cocina, sala de estar, estudio, biblioteca, capilla, y una zona privada, incluyendo las diez viviendas individuales. Basado en los principios simples de luz, sombra y orientación, el diseõ de la forma de la casa esta determinada por el clima y la función donde muchos de los espacios tienen una relación singular a la luz.

D **Die Brophy-Jesuiten**-Gemeinde erteilte den Auftrag, ein neues Wohngebäude für zehn Priester zu entwerfen. Die zwei auf dem Grundstück wachsenden, weiß blühenden Oleander-hecken dienten dabei als Inspirationsquelle. Das Raumpro-gramm umfasst eine Gemeinschaftszone mit Küche, Wohn-zimmer, Studierzimmer, Bibliothek und Kapelle sowie einen privaten Bereich mit einzelnen Wohnungen. Durch die Verwen-dung einfacher Prinzipien von Licht, Schatten und Raumaus-richtung wird den klimatischen Gegebenheiten und funktio-nalen Notwendigkeiten Rechnung getragen.

F **Commandé par la** Communauté Jésuite de Brophy qui avait besoin d'un nouveau foyer pour dix prêtres jésuites, le projet tire son inspiration des deux bordures de laurier-rose à fleur blanches déjà existantes. Le projet de la résidence néces-sitait de disposer d'une zone publique, comprenant la cuisine, la salle de séjour, le bureau, la bibliothèque et la chapelle, et d'une zone privée, comprenant les dix logements individuels. Basée sur les principes simples de la lumière, de l'ombre et de l'orientation, la maison est dessinée par le climat et sa fonc-tion, et beaucoup des espaces ont une relation particulière avec la lumière.

Project City Phoenix (AZ)
Typology Living
Completion Year 2003
Photos Bill Timmerman Photography

02 Garden view

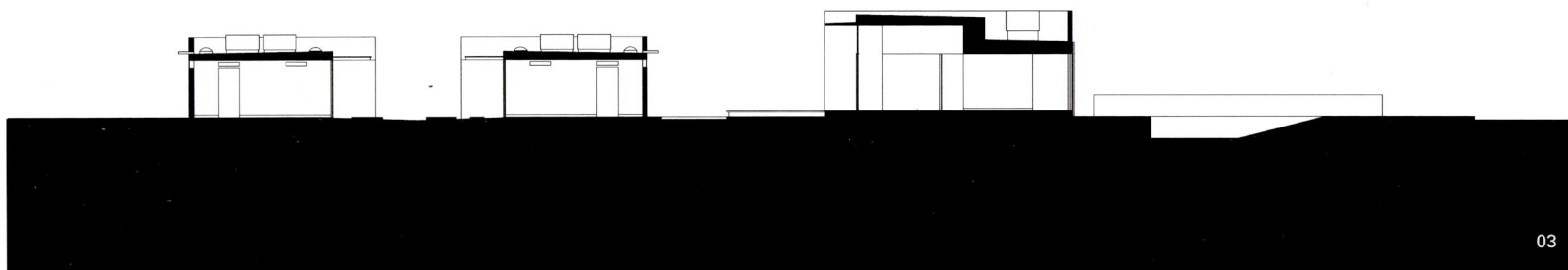

03 Section
04 Public zone: living room
05 Exterior view by dawn

06 Floor plans
07 View to garden

06

07

PRAYER PAVILION OF LIGHT

01

01 Exterior view by night

E **The Prayer Pavilion** of Light is part of a large church campus in Phoenix, Arizona. Sited along the edge of a desert preserve, a series of inclined planes are incised by a long processional walk, revealing the orthogonal chapel as one gradually ascends the 28-foot vertical between the chapel mount and garden entrance. Arrival upon the exposed-aggregate plaza, one is met with an orderly, yet inviting bosque of desert trees and a black reflection pool. Emerging from the water, a flame burns adjacent to a 50 foot-high steel cross.

ES **El Prayer Pavilion** of Light forma parte de un campus de iglesia grande en Phoenix, Arizona. Ubicado a lo largo del borde de un vedado de desierto, una serie de superficies inclinadas se dividen por un paseo processional largo, revelando la capilla ortogonal al ascender gradualmente los 8,5 metros verticales entre el montaje de la capilla y la entrada del jardín. Al llegar a la plaza incorporada expuesta, se encuentra un bosque de árboles de desierto y un estanque de agua reflexión negro; de la cual surge una llama que se quema adyacente a una cruz de acero de 15 metros de altura.

D **Der Pavillon ist** Teil eines weitläufigen Kirchengeländes am Rande eines Wüstenschutzgebietes. Mehrere schräge Ebenen werden durch einen langen Prozessionsweg eingeschnitten. Dieser führt zu der rechtwinklig angelegten Kapelle – nach einem achteinhalb Meter hohen Anstieg zwischen dem Kapellhügel und dem Garteneingang. Oben, auf einem Platz, findet sich der Besucher in einem gepflegten Wüstenwäldchen mit einem schwarzen Becken wieder. Aus diesem ragt eine brennende Flamme neben dem 15 Meter hohen Kreuz aus Stahl.

F **Le projet fait** partie du grand campus d'une église à Phoenix, Arizona. Situé en lisière d'une réserve désertique, il présente une série de plans inclinés incisés par une longue promenade processionnelle, révélant la chapelle orthogonale au fur et à mesure que l'on monte les 8,5 mètre qui séparent la colline de la chapelle et de l'entrée du jardin. Une fois arrivé sur la place de graviers, on fait face à des arbres du désert, agencés de manière formelle mais séduisante, ainsi qu'à un bassin aux reflets noirs. Emergeant de l'eau, une flamme brûle près d'une croix d'acier de 15 mètre de haut.

USA

DE BARTOLO ARCHITECTS

Project City Phoenix (AZ)
Typology Culture
Completion Year 2007
Photos Bill Timmerman Photography

02 Planted courtyard

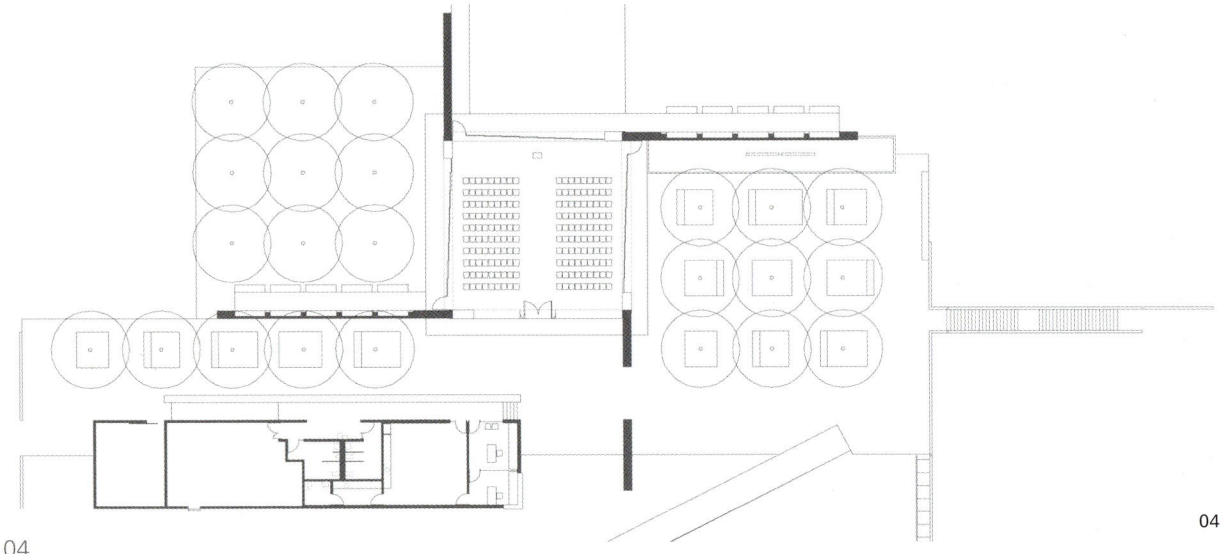

03

04

03 Inner/outdoor praying area
04 Floor plan
05 View inside chapel
06 Detail processional walk
07 Detail steel cross, emerging from the water of the black reflection pool

05

06

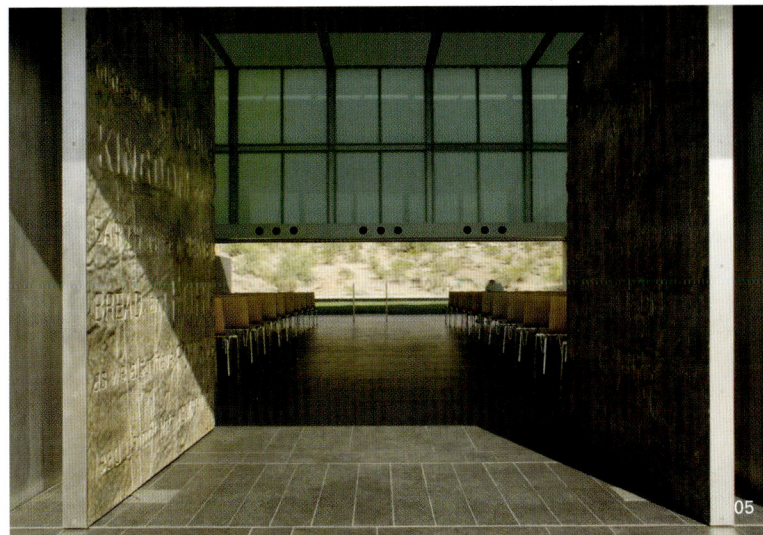

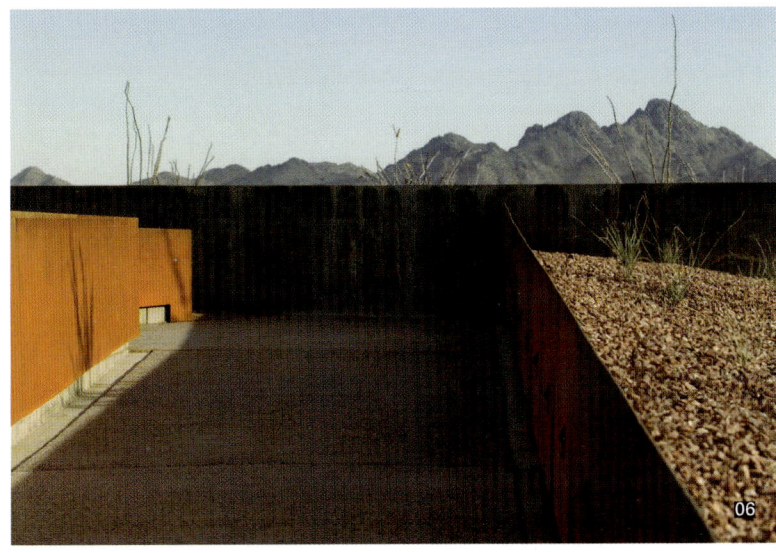

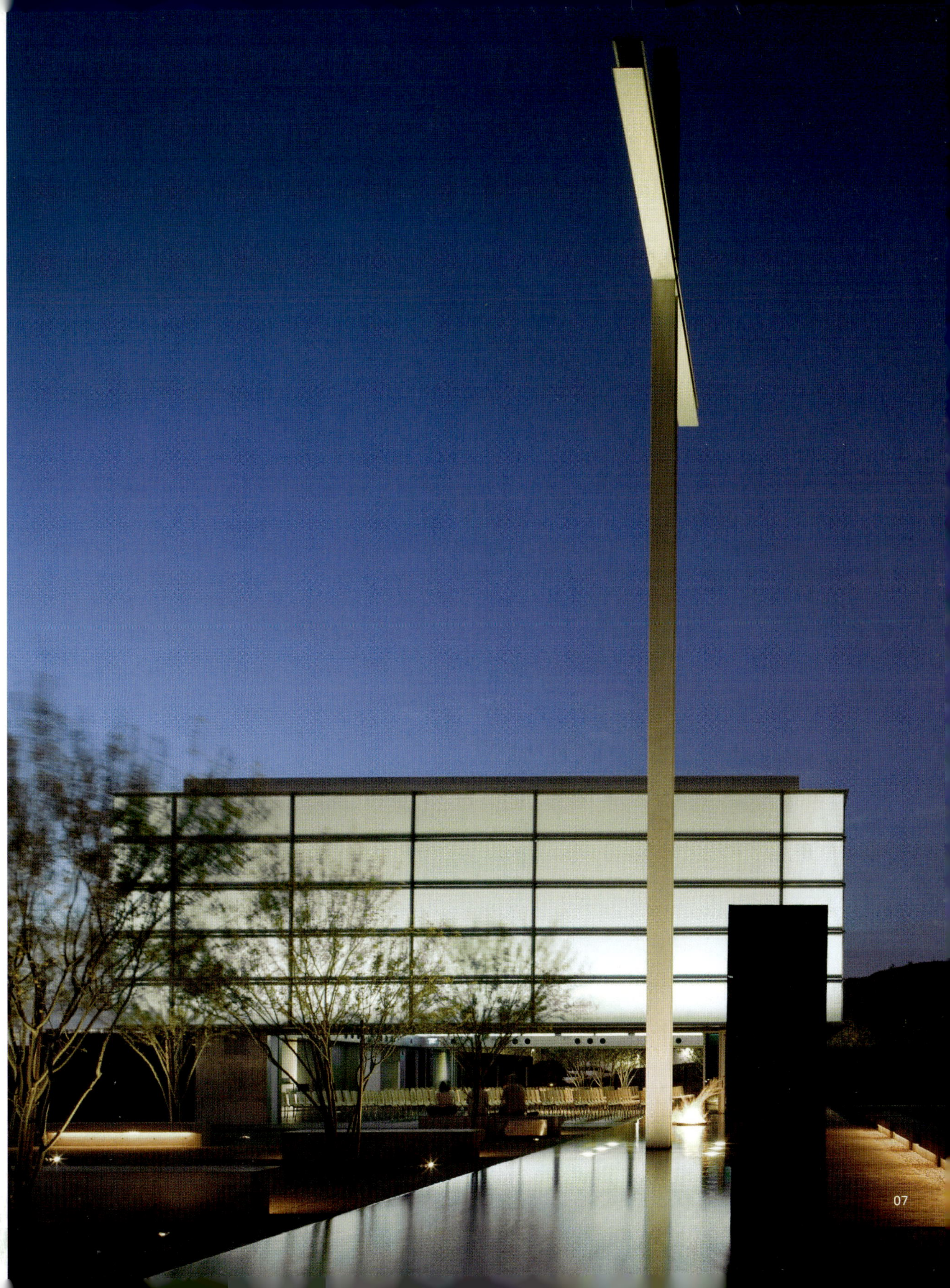
07

08

08 Illuminated exterior by night
09 View into the free-ventilated praying area

CITY OF PHOENIX NEIGHBOR-HOOD RESOURCE CENTER

01 Street side view

USA

MARLENE IMIRZIAN & ASSOCIATES ARCHITECTS

E   **The Neighborhood Resource** Center (NRC) is an outpost for city services, modest in scale and budget, but creating a strong presence. In recognition of the desert climate, the NRC is a courtyard building oriented in the east-west axis. The form recalls the many nearby industrial sheds, with a palate of metal siding and standard block; simple shed forms are extruded along block boxes. Abundant glazing along the street façade, entries, and community rooms permits the building to act as a "pair of eyes" on the community.

ES   **El Neighborhood Resource** Center (NRC) es un puesto avanzado para servicios de la ciudad, modesto en escala y presupuesto, pero creando una presencia fuerte. En reconocimiento al clima de desierto, el NRC es un edificio con patios que se orientadan hacia el eje Este-Oeste. La forma recuerda muchos cobertizos cercanos industriales, con una cubierta de apartadero metálico y el bloque estándar; formas de cobertizo simples son expulsadas a lo largo de cajas de bloque. Cristales abundantes a lo largo de la fachada de la calle, entradas, y salones de comunidad permiten al edificio actuar como "un par de ojos" sobre la comunidad.

D   **Das Zentrum ist** eine Außenstelle für die städtischen Versorgungsdienste, zurückhaltend hinsichtlich Größe und Budget, aber dennoch mit einer starken Präsenz. Im Hinblick auf das Wüstenklima wurde ein Hofgebäude mit Ost-West-Ausrichtung entworfen. Die Form greift die zahlreichen Industriehallen ringsum durch die Metallverschalung auf. Die großzügige Verglasung der Straßenfassade, der Eingänge und der Gemeinschaftsräume lässt das Gebäude gleichsam wie ein „Augenpaar" auf die Gemeinde schauen.

F   **Le Neighborhood Resource** Center (NRC) est un avant-poste pour les services municipaux, modeste en échelle et en budget, mais à la présence forte. Conçu spécialement pour le climat du désert, le NRC est un bâtiment avec cour intérieure orienté selon un axe est-ouest. Sa forme rappelle les nombreux hangars industriels voisins, avec son bardage métallique et aspect bloc ; les formes simples sont profilées le long des blocs. Les nombreuses vitres le long de la façade côté rue, les entrées et les salles communes permettent au bâtiment d'agir un peu comme une paire d'yeux sur la communauté.

Project City Phoenix (AZ)
Typology Public
Completion Year 2006
Photos Bill Timmerman Photography

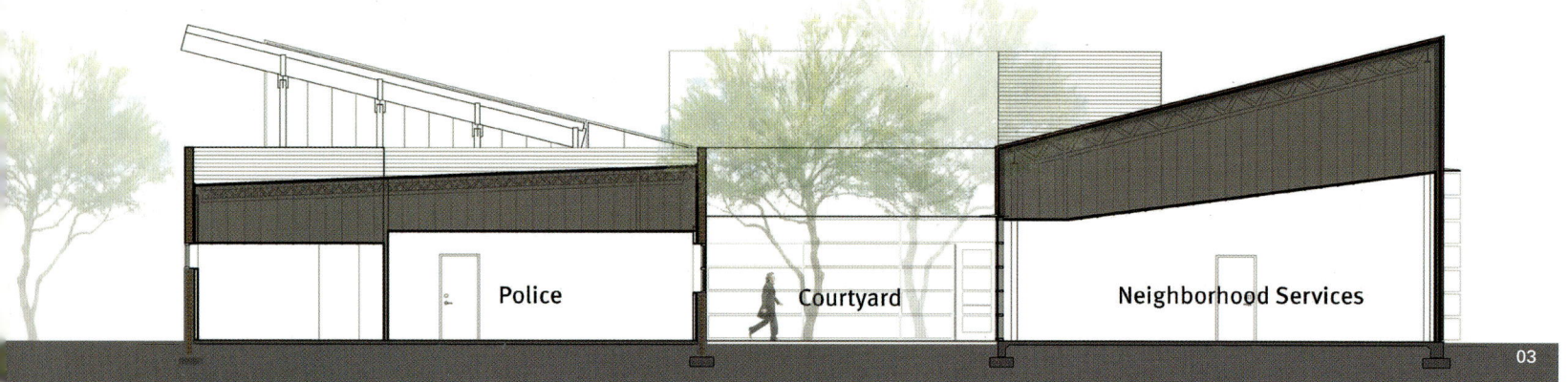

Police

Courtyard

Neighborhood Services

03

04

NEIGHBORHOOD
RESOURCE
CENTER

05

HOTEL VALLEY HO

01

01 View inside lobby

USA

ALLEN + PHILP ARCHITECTS / INTERIORS

E **Preservation, reuse and** celebration are the design themes used in renovating and adding on to this historic hotel. Noted for its organic architectural style with a "southwestern" character that bridged modern and western detailing, new retro-contemporary elements are featured including a perfectly circular pool defining the space, with private cabanas and a dramatic fire and fountain feature. The most spectacular addition is a seven-story tower that contains a spa and fitness center and five levels of condominium residences.

ES **La preservación, reutilización** y celebración son los temas de diseño usados en la renovacion y añadidura a este hotel histórico. Caracterizdo por su estilo orgánico arquitectónico con un carácter "del sudoeste" que acortó el detallar moderno y occidental; destacan nuevos elementos retro-contemporáneos incluyendo una piscina perfectamente circular que define el espacio, con cabañas privadas y una chimenea y fuente espectacular. El aditamento más espectacular es una torre de siete niveles que contiene un spa y un centro de bienestar, junto con cinco niveles de pisos habitacionales.

D **Erhaltung, Wiedernutzbarmachung und** Wertschätzung sind die Entwurfsthemen der Sanierung und Erweiterung dieses historischen Hotels. Vielbeachtet wegen seiner organischen Architektur, die moderne mit typisch westlichen Details verbindet, weist es neue Retro-Elemente auf, wie etwa einen kreisrunden Pool mit privaten Hütten und einer spektakulären Feuerstelle nebst Springbrunnen. Die wohl aufregendste Ergänzung ist ein siebenstöckiger Turm, der ein Spa und ein Fitness-Center beherbergt sowie Eigentumswohnungen auf fünf Etagen.

F **Préservation, réutilisation et** célébration sont les mots clés de la rénovation et de l'extension de cet hôtel historique. Remarqué pour son style architectural organique avec un caractère « du sud-ouest » qui fait le lien entre les détails modernes et western, il comprend des éléments nouveaux rétro-contemporains, notamment une piscine parfaitement circulaire définissant l'espace, avec des cabines privées et un jeu spectaculaire d'eau et de feu. L'addition la plus spectaculaire est une tour de sept étages qui contient un spa et un centre de fitness et cinq niveaux de résidences en copropriété.

Project City Scottsdale (AZ)
Typology Hospitality
Completion Year 2005
Photos Bill Timmerman Photography, Mark Boisclair (02)

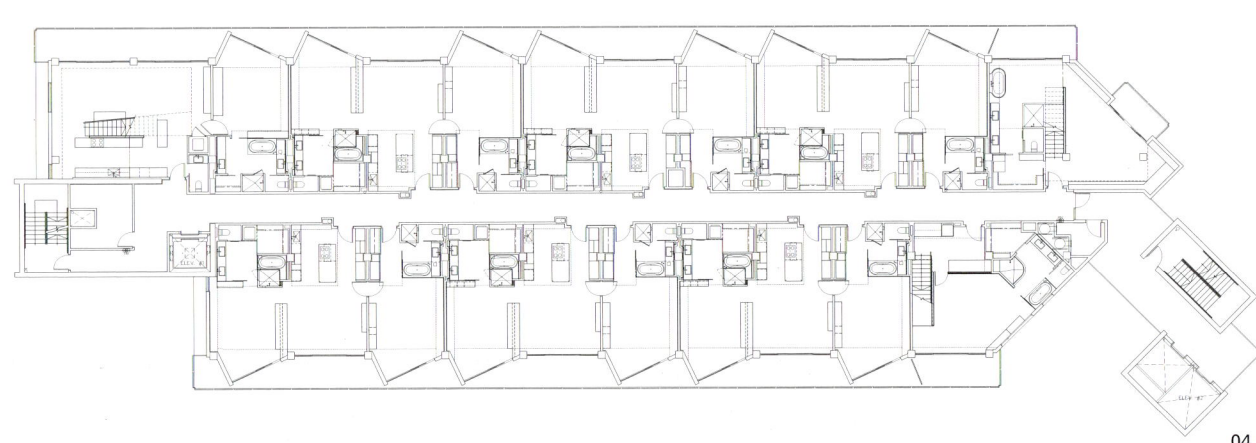

03 Lounge with fireplace
04 Typical guest room floor plan
05 Detail façade
06 Courtyard

07 View into guest rooms with terraces

THE DUKE

01

01 Exterior view by night

E **The Duke is** an urban desert, comprised of eight attached town homes. The modern, pure building cuts a clean sharp edge through the randomly built environment of the surrounding area. Compact and efficient, emphasis was placed on sustainable design through successfully participating in Scottsdale's Residential Green Building Program. The Duke's intent is to express individuality as a singular building with eight individual homeowners, while promoting community through architectural transparency on the second floor.

ES **The Duke es** un desierto urbano, conformado de ocho casas unifamiliar agrupadas. El edificio moderno y puro atraviesa un ambiente construido naturalmente del área circundante para emplazarse nitidamente. Compacto y eficiente, el enfoque se hizo en el diseño sostenible participando satisfactoriamente en el Programa de Edificio Residencial Verde de Scottsdale. La intención del Duke es de expresar la individualidad como un edificio singular con ocho propietarios individuales, promoviendo la conexión con la comunidad con la transparencia arquitectónica de la segunda planta.

D **The Duke besteht** aus acht miteinander verbundenen Stadthäusern. Das moderne, puristische Projekt bildet einen scharfen Schnitt durch die eher belanglose und banale Bebauung der Umgebung. Der Fokus richtet sich auf einen nachhaltigen Entwurf, der sich auch in der erfolgreichen Teilnahme am „Scottsdale's Residential Green Building Program" widerspiegelt. The Duke zeugt gleichermaßen von Individualität der acht verschiedenen Besitzer wie von Gemeinschaft, welche in der transparenten Gestaltung des zweiten Stockwerks ihren Ausdruck findet.

F **The Duke est** un apport urbain dans le désert, comprenant huit maisons de villes mitoyennes. La construction moderne, pure, découpe un angle net à travers l'environnement chaotique de cette zone. Compact et efficace, le design met l'accent sur le développement durable en participant avec succès au Programme de Construction Résidentielle Vert de Scottsdale. L'intention de The Duke est d'exprimer l'individualité, en tant que bâtiment autonome ayant huit propriétaires différents, tout en promouvant la communauté grâce à la transparence architecturale du deuxième étage.

USA
CIRCLE WEST ARCHITECTURE

Project City Scottsdale (AZ)
Typology Living
Completion Year 2006
Photos Rieser Photography

02 Street view

03 Kitchen
04 Façade detail
05 Exterior view

SCOTTSDALE FIRST ASSEMBLY

01

01 Exterior view

E **This masonry structure** is a regional church, along with administration and classroom spaces. It represents the first phase of a long-range architectural plan composed of masonry planes, weathered metal and glass. From the entry plaza the various programs pivot from the central lobby and worship space, where the linear arrangement of offices and classrooms foreshadow the future growth of the campus. The structures are organized around an existing natural wash, diagonally bisecting the site.

ES **Esta estructura de** albañilería es una iglesia regional, con espacios administrativos y de aula. Representa la primera fase de un plan arquitectónico de largo alcance compuesto de superficies de albañilería, metal desgastado y cristal. De la plaza de entrada varios programas giran del vestíbulo central y el espacio de adoración, donde el orden lineal de oficinas y aulas presagia el futuro crecimiento del campus. Las estructuras estan organizadas alrededor de una existencia de un suelo natural, en diagonal bisecando el solar.

D **Dieser Mauerwerksbau ist** ein Kirchengebäude mit angeschlossenen Verwaltungs- und Klassenräumen. Er stellt die erste Phase eines langfristigen Entwicklungsprojektes dar und besteht aus gemauerten Flächen, verwittertem Metall und Glas. Vom Eingang her ziehen sich die verschiedenen Räume kreisförmig von der zentralen Vorhalle über den eigentlichen Kirchenraum, von dem die lineare Anordnung von Büros und Klassenzimmern das zukünftige Wachsen des Campus erahnen lassen. Ein Graben, der das Gelände durchschneidet, strukturiert den Komplex.

F **Cette structure de** maçonnerie est une église régionale, disposant également d'espaces administratifs et d'enseignement. Elle représente la première phase d'un plan architectural de longue portée comportant des bâtiments en maçonnerie, en verre et en métal qui se patinera avec le temps. Depuis la place d'entrée, les différents programmes pivotent depuis le hall central et l'espace de prière, où l'agencement linéaire des bureaux et des salles de classe présagent de la croissance future du campus. Les structures sont organisées autour d'un oued naturel existant, qui divise le site en diagonale.

USA

DE BARTOLO ARCHITECTS

Project City Scottsdale (AZ)
Typology Culture
Completion Year 2005
Photos Bill Timmerman Photography

02 Weathered metal and glass façade

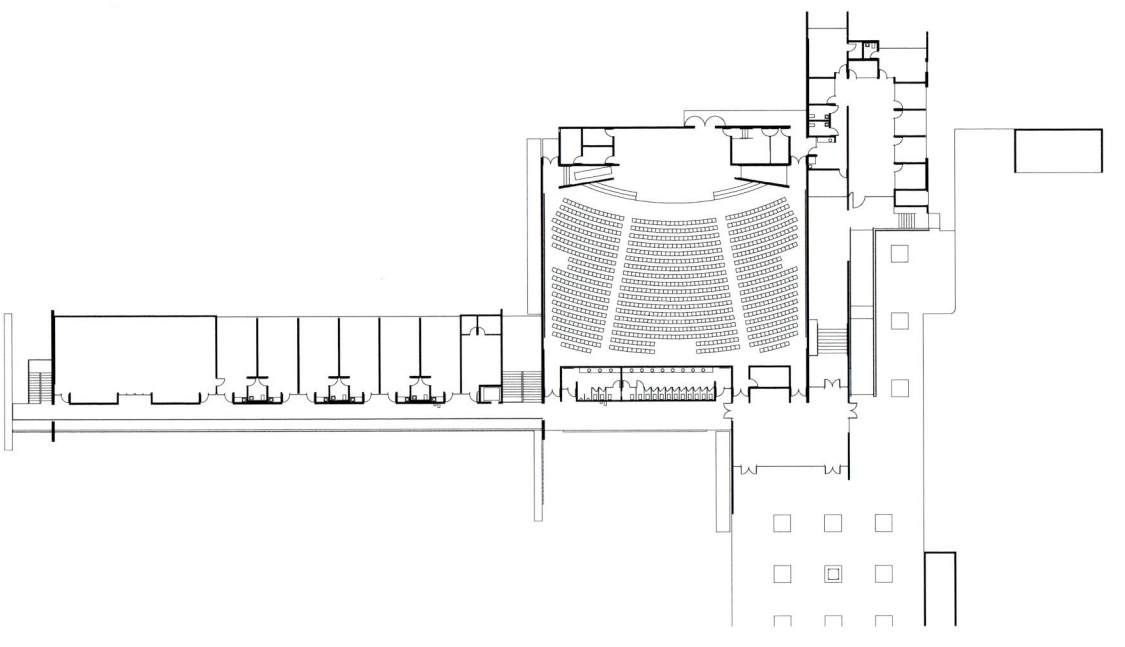

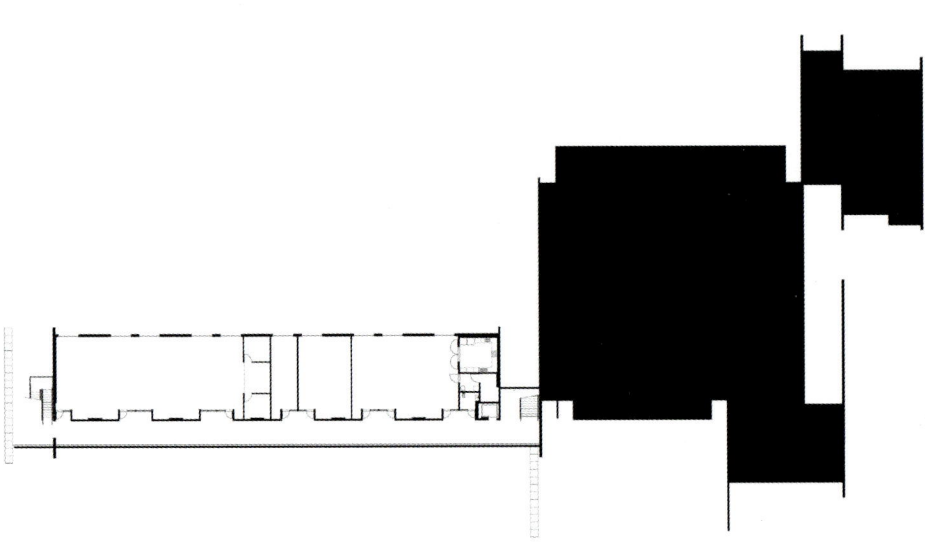

03 Floor plans
04 Rear view
05 Interior assembly hall

06 Courtyard
07 Rear view

ARABIAN PUBLIC LIBRARY

01

01 View into courtyard

E **As a remembrance of** the desert slot canyons found in northern Arizona and monument valley, the Arabian Public Library captures the powerful and unique experience of being caught in between compressive stone walls and the ultimate release of sky above. Ever-patient threads of water sculpt and polish the walls, cutting the natural sandstone canyons over millennia. Harder stone and slow water sharply define vertical slivers while softer stone gives way to wider crevasse. The library echoes this powerful sequence of the desertscape.

ES **Como una remembranza** de los cañones de ranura de desierto encontrados en Arizona del norte y el valle de monumento, la Arabian Public Library (Biblioteca Publica Arabe) captura la experiencia poderosa y única de ser cogido en medio de paredes compresivas de piedra y la liberación última de cielo encima. Las paredes son esculpidas y pulidas por agua, que corta los cañones de arenisca naturales sobre milenarios. Piedras mas duras y agua bruscamente definen astillas verticales mientras la piedra más suave cede el paso a la más amplia hendidura. La biblioteca repite esta secuencia poderosa del paisaje del desierto.

D **Die Bibliothek reflektiert** und interpretiert das Eingesperrtsein zwischen erdrückenden Steinmauern und der ultimativen Freiheit des Himmels; das Bauwerk erinnert dabei an die Desert Slot Canyons in Nord-Arizona und im Monument Valley. Immerfließende „Wasserfäden" haben die natürlichen Sandstein-Canyons über die Jahrtausende geformt und abgeschliffen. Härterer Stein und langsame Wasser-Fließgeschwindigkeit schaffen scharfe vertikale Einschnitte, während weicherer Stein Raum für breitere Spalten lässt. Diese Naturgegebenheiten finden in der Architektur ihre Entsprechung.

F **Comme une réminiscence** des canyons du désert du nord de l'Arizona et de Monument Valley, l'Arabian Public Library retranscrit cette expérience puissante et unique d'être coincé entre des murs de pierre oppressants et le ciel. Des gouttes d'eau ont patiemment sculpté et poli les murs, dessinant les canyons de grès naturels pendant un millénaire. Des tranches verticales ont été découpées par la pierre plus dure et le ruissellement de l'eau, tandis que les pierres plus friables ont permis la formation d'une crevasse plus profonde. La Bibliothèque fait écho à cette puissance du désert.

USA
RICHÄRD+BAUER

Project City Scottsdale (AZ)
Typology Public
Completion Year 2007
Photos Bill Timmerman Photography, Mark Boisclair (04, 06)

03 Entry view
04 Outdoor sitting area
05 Site plan

Loop Road

07 Reading room with view to courtyard
08 Hallway
09 Façade detail

3 DESERT WAY

01

01 Exterior view by dawn

E   **The project,** 3 Desert Way or Desert Shelter, is a student living and study space designed, built and lived in by Trevor Pan at Taliesin West; the western home and school of Frank Lloyd Wright. A natural approach to environmental controls has been achieved with site orientation, operable windows, louvers, cross ventilation and natural lighting. Pre-fabricated parts and concrete forms were made in the school's shop, assembled on-site to minimize impact on the desert, while no commercial concrete trucks were employed.

ES   **El proyecto,** 3 Desert Way o Desert Shelter (Refugio de Desierto), es una vivienda y espacio de estudio estudiantil diseñado y construido cerca del Trevor Pan en el Oeste Taliesin; la casa occidental y escuela de Frank Lloyd Wright. La propuesta natural a mandos ambientales fue lograda con la orientación del emplazamiento, ventanas operables, persianas, ventilación cruzada y la iluminación natural. Para reducir al mínimo el impacto sobre el desierto, elementos prefabricados y hormigón fueron fabricados en la escuela y montados en el emplazamiento, eliminando el uso de camiones comerciales para transportar el hormigón por completo.

D   **Das Projekt ist** Wohn- und Arbeitsraum für Studierende in Taliesin West. Es wurde von dem Architekten nicht nur entworfen und gebaut, sondern wird auch von ihm bewohnt. Der Bau ist eine naturbezogene Annäherung an einen umweltgerechten Baustil durch die Nutzung der Grundstücks-Ausrichtung, Fenster die zu öffnen sind, Jalousien, Querlüftung und natürlicher Beleuchtung. Vorgefertigte Teile und Betonformen wurden in der Werkstatt der Schule hergestellt und vor Ort zusammengesetzt – auch eine Maßnahme um die Umwelt weitestgehend zu schonen.

F   **Ce projet,** 3 Desert Way ou Desert Shelter, est un espace de vie et d'études pour étudiants conçu, construit et habité par Trevor Pan à Taliesin West, la maison et l'école de Frank Lloyd Wright. Une approche naturelle des contrôles environnementaux a été permise grâce à l'orientation du site, des fenêtres et des persiennes, une aération transversale et un éclairage naturel. Des parties préfabriquées et des formes en béton ont été fabriquées dans l'atelier de l'école, assemblées sur site pour minimiser l'impact sur le désert, et aucun camion-bétonnière du commerce n'a été utilisé.

USA
TREVOR PAN

Project City Scottsdale (AZ)
Typology Living
Completion Year 2006
Photos Jerry Portelli

02　Exterior view of operable windows and louvers

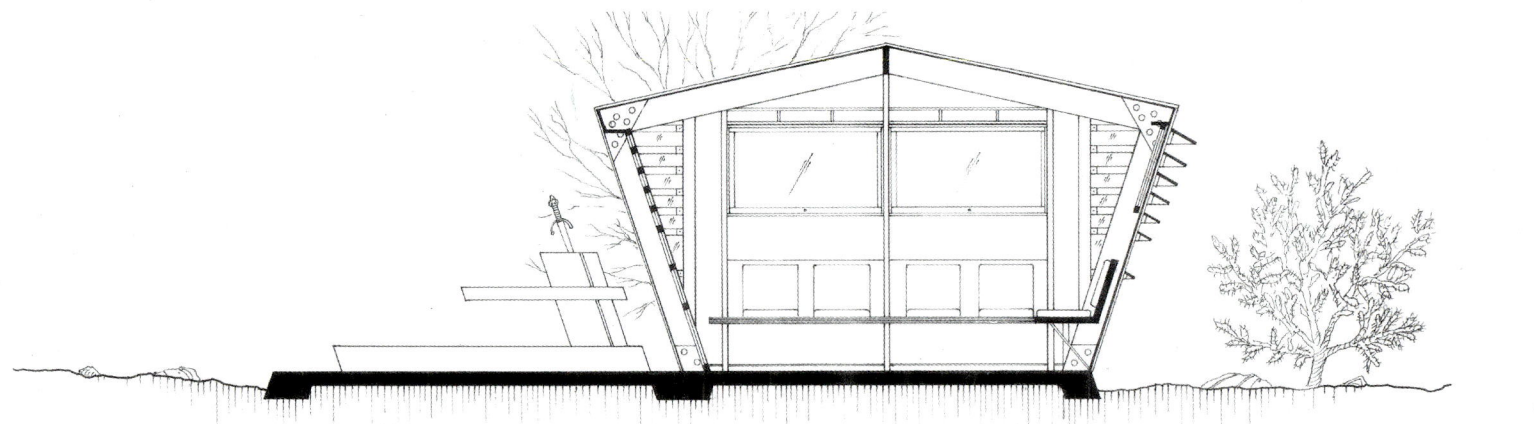

03

03 Section
04 Interior seating
05 Exterior view
06 Outdoor area extending to landscape

04

05

LUNA ROSSA

01 Curved pool and sun deck

E   **This house uses** every available surface to maximize the potential of the lot. Built on a 2.06-acre lot with unobstructed views of Boynton Canyon and Cockscomb, bordering the National forest, Luna Rossa is nestled among ancient junipers and tall pinions. Featuring an expansive floor plan with vast rooms facing the pool in circular motion, while the unobstrusive, functional elegance of the living areas revolve around a private internal garden.

ES   **Esta casa usa** cada una de sus superficies para maximizar el potencial del solar. Construida en un emplazamiento de 8.000 con vistas despejadas del Cañón Boynton y Cockscomb, lindando con el bosque Nacional, Luna Rossa se recosta entre enebros antiguos y altos piñones. La casa consiste en un plano amplio con espacios enormes que afrontan la piscina en un movimiento circular, mientras la elegancia funcional ininterrumpida de las diferentes superficies de la casa gira alrededor de un jardín privado interno.

D   **Weite Räume orientieren** sich in einer Kreisbewegung hin zu einem Pool, während sich die Wohnräume in funktionaler Eleganz um einen privaten inneren Garten gruppieren und einen kontinuierlichen offenen Fluss zwischen allen Räumen ermöglichen. Die Master-Suite liegt abseits der übrigen Zimmer. Die offene Küche verbindet eine hochwertige Ausstattung mit bestem italienischen Design.

F   **Cette maison utilise** toute la surface disponible pour augmenter le potentiel du terrain. Construite sur un terrain de 8000 mètre carré, avec une vue totalement dégagée sur le Canyon de Boynton et Cockscomb, tout près d'une forêt nationale, Luna Rossa est nichée parmi de vieux genévriers et de hauts pignons. Elle dispose d'un vaste plan au sol avec de grandes pièces faisant face à la piscine dans un mouvement circulaire, et les espaces de vie à l'élégance discrète et fonctionnelle tournent autour d'un jardin intérieur privé.

USA

SANBA ARCHITECTURE

Project City Sedona (AZ)
Typology Living
Completion Year 2007
Photos Blacky Schwartz

02 Interior glass-encased pond

03

04

05

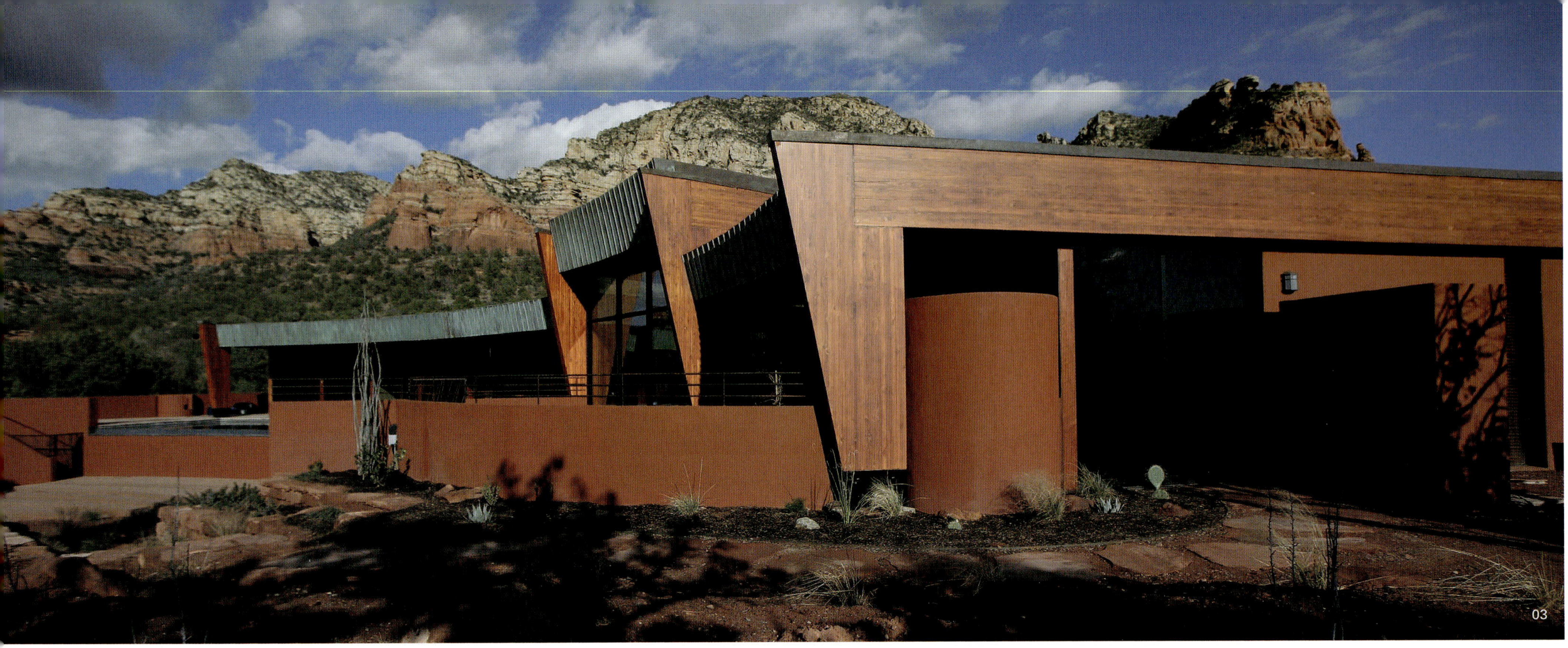

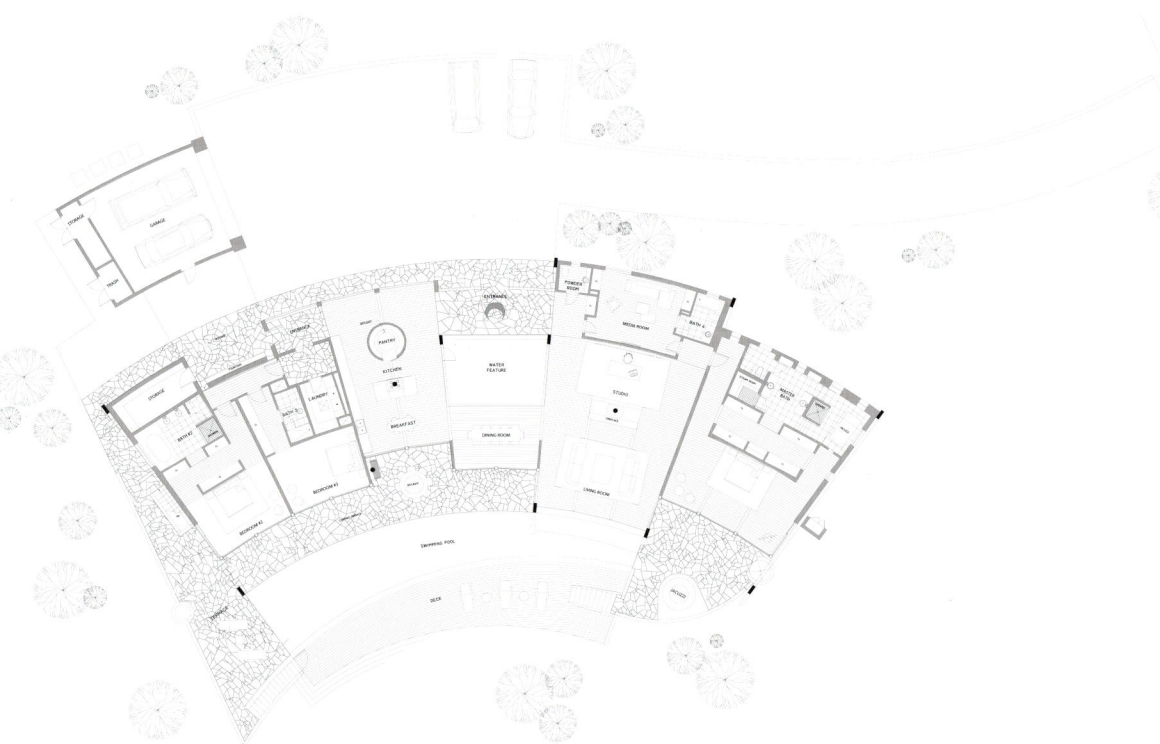

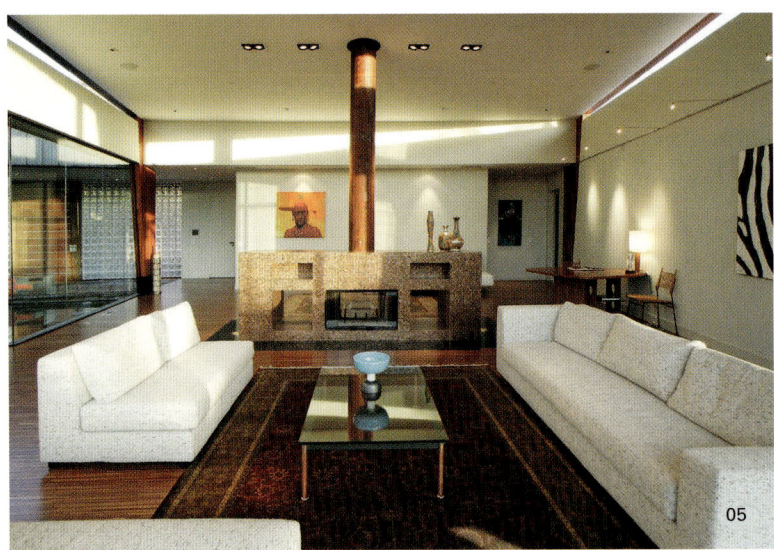

03 Exterior view façade
04 Site plan
05 Living space with fireplace

06   Bowed pool and view inside living space

PARCEL 7A, LONGBOW BUSINESS PARK

E   **The overall design** objective of the Longbow Parcel 7 development was to approach the unique qualities of designing in the Sonoran Desert in a manner that is organic and expressive. Within the project, the office building is characterized by a long narrow site that led to the development of a building that contains vertically design "light courts" cut into the elongated office floor plates. The plan of the building is bowed, gently curved, and moves out towards the south becoming slightly larger on the upper floors.

ES   **El objetivo del** diseño total del desarrollo de Longbow Parcel 7 se aproxima a las calidades únicas de diseñar en el Desierto de Sonoran, en una manera orgánica y expresiva. Dentro del proyecto, el edificio de oficinas es caracterizado por su estrecho emplazamiento que condujo al desarrollo de un espacio que contiene " patios de luz " organizados verticalmente dividiendo los pisos de oficinas alargados. La planta del edificio se encorva delicadamente, y se mueve hacia el sur convirtiendo los niveles superiores en espacios mas amplios.

D   **Das prinzipielle Entwurfsziel** des Bauprojektes war es, sich den besonderen Bedingungen der Sonora-Wüste in einer organischen und gleichzeitig expressiven Weise zu nähern. Der Baugrund für das Bürogebäude ist lang und schmal, weshalb die Architekten einen Bau mit vertikal geführten Lichthöfen entwarfen, welche in die lang gestreckten Geschossplatten quasi eingeschnitten sind. Der bogenförmige Grundriss des Gebäudes zieht sich nach Süden hin und erweitert sich leicht in den oberen Geschossen.

F   **L'objectif général** de Longbow Parcel 7 était d'aborder d'une manière organique et expressive les qualités singulières d'une architecture dans le désert de Sonoran Desert. Au sein du projet, l'immeuble de bureau est caractérisé par un long site étroit, qui a mené à l'élaboration d'un bâtiment contenant des « cours de lumières » verticales découpées dans les plaques de plancher du bureau. Le plan du bâtiment est légèrement incurvé et se déplace vers le sud, en devenant légèrement plus large aux étages supérieurs.

01

01 Exterior view from street side

USA

CIRCLE WEST ARCHITECTS

Project City Mesa (AZ)
Typology Office
Completion Year unrealized
Renderings Circle West Architects

02 Fully glazed façade by night

03 Exterior view
04 Curved façade
05 Rear view with courtyard
06 Planted courtyard
07 Building elevation

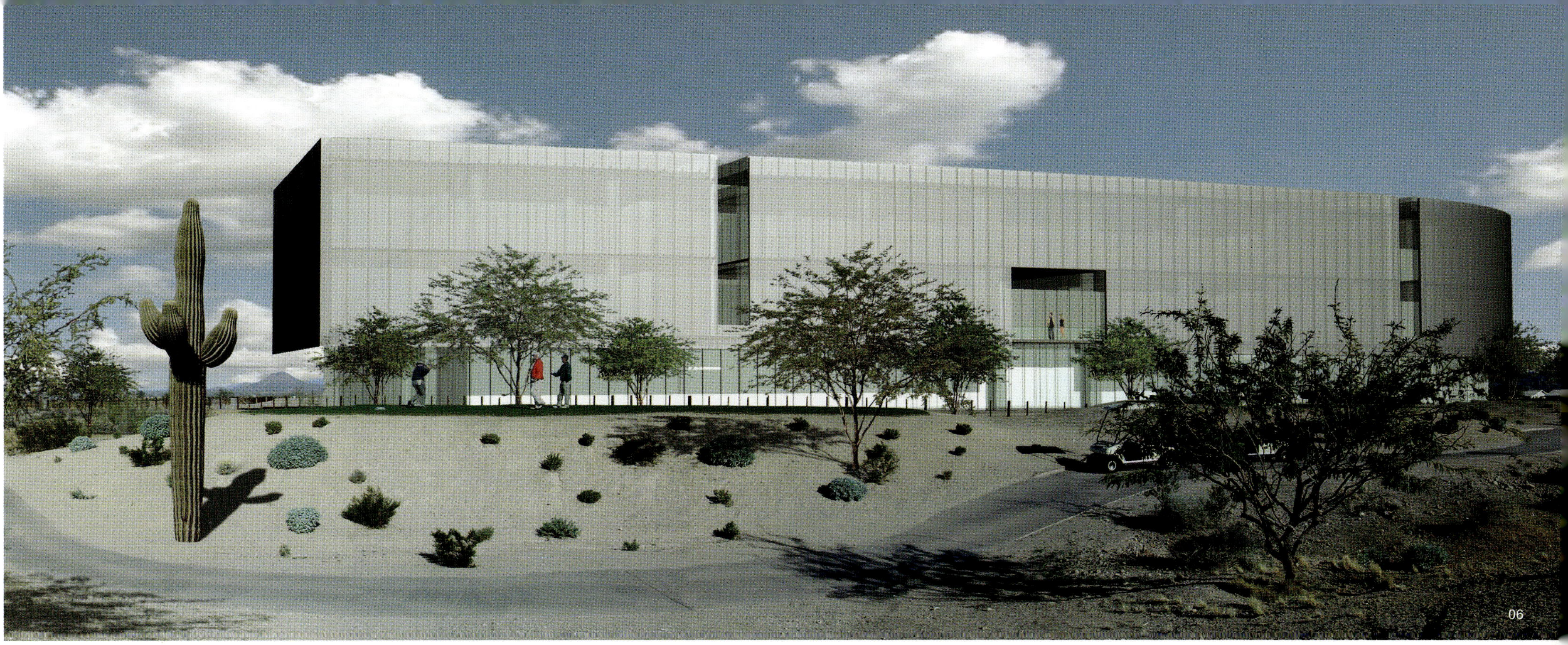
06

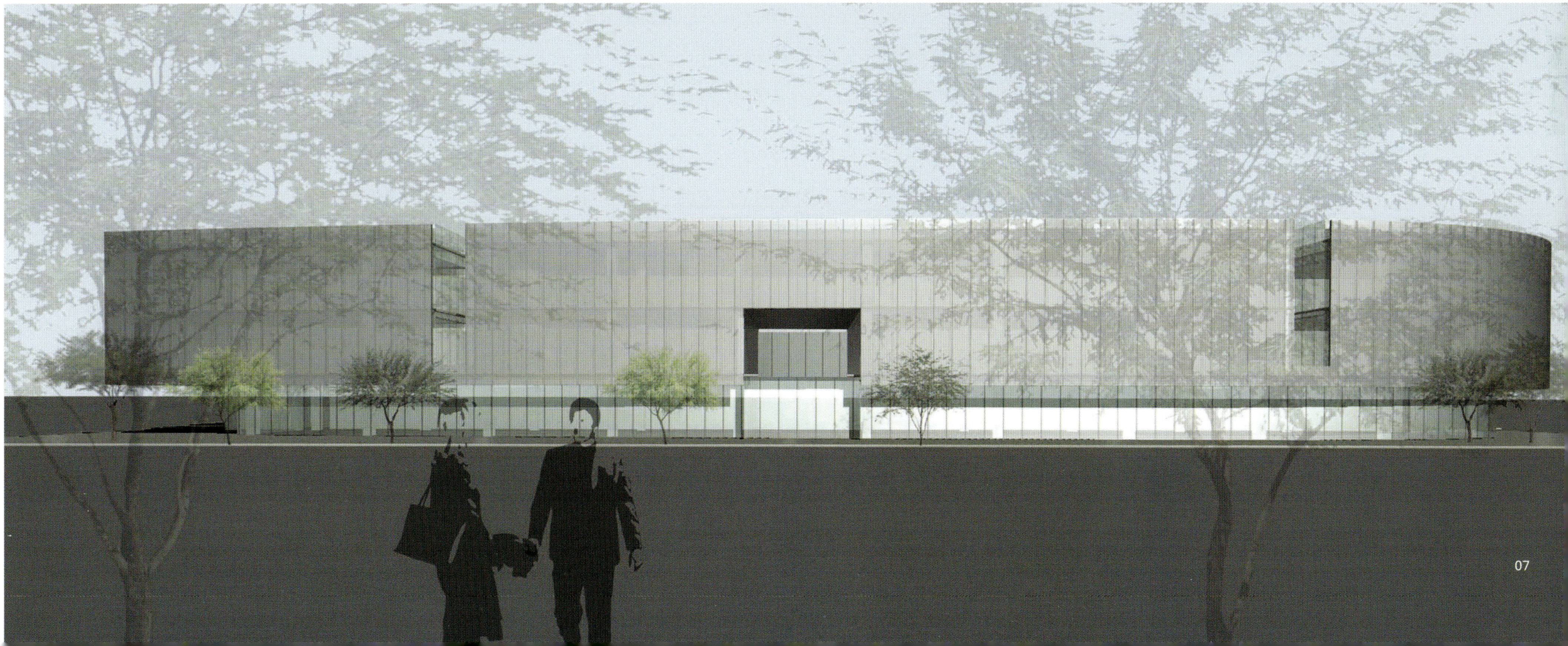
07

SOCIAL CONDENSER FOR SUPERIOR

01 Entrance area

E **The Social Condenser** is a mixed-use building located at the base of the Superstition Mountain Range. The project is a renovation and expansion of an existing two-story building, as well as an addition of an exterior dining terrace. Classically an obscured, introverted diagram, the Social Condenser aims to balance concealment with exuberant exposure of the internal activities. It is envisioned to be the living room of the community in order to serve as a place to congregate and view work of local artists.

ES **El Social Condenser** es una edificación de multiples usos localizado en la base de la Sierra de Superstición. El proyecto es una renovación y extensión de un edificio existente de dos plantas, así como una adición de una terraza exterior para comer. Tradicionalmente un diagrama obscurecido, introvertido, el Social Condenser pretende crear un equilibrio entre lo oculto con la exposición exuberante de las actividades internas. Esta previsto ser el salon de la comunidad y ser un lugar para congregar y exponer el trabajo de artistas de la zona.

D **Der „Social Condenser"** ist am Fuße des Gebirgszugs „Superstition" (Aberglaube) gelegen. Bei dem Bauvorhaben handelt es sich um die Sanierung und Erweiterung eines zweistöckigen Gebäudes, welches um eine Außenterrasse ergänzt wurde. Eigentlich mit einem verborgenen, nach innen gerichteten Bauplan ausgestattet, zielt das Projekt auf den Ausgleich zwischen Verborgenheit und Enthüllung dessen ab, was sich im Innern abspielt. So soll das Projekt als eine Art „Wohnzimmer für die Gemeinschaft" dienen, in dem man sich zu den verschiedensten An-lässen versammelt.

F **Le Social Condenser** est un bâtiment d'utilisation mixte situé au pied de la chaîne de montagnes Superstition. Le projet est une rénovation et une extension d'un bâtiment sur deux niveaux existant, ainsi que l'adjonction d'une terrasse extérieure avec salle à manger. Comme un diagramme obscurci, introverti et classique, le Social Condenser cherche à équilibrer son aspect caché avec l'exposition exubérante de ses activités internes. Il est conçu pour être le salon de la communauté et pour servir de lieu de rencontre et de découverte des œuvres d'artistes locaux.

USA

BLANK STUDIO

Project City Superior (AZ)
Typology Culture/Public
Completion Year 2007
Photos Bill Timmerman Photography

02 Exterior view and courtyard

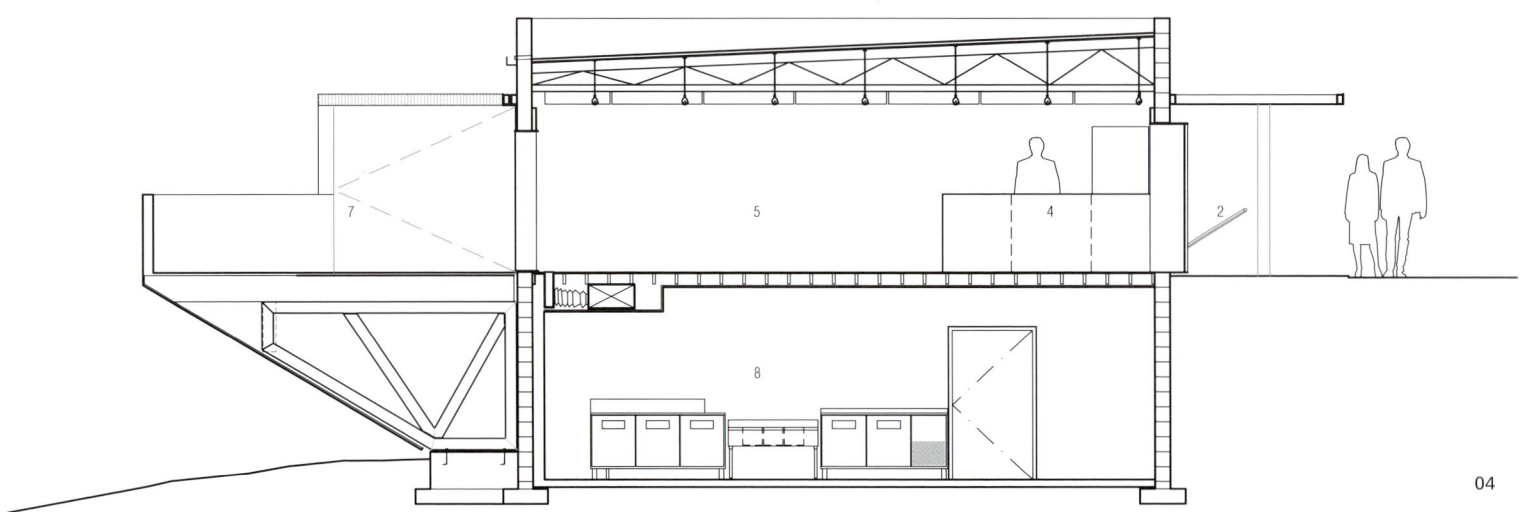

03

04

05

06

03 Courtyard
04 Section
05 Main floor plan
06 Exterior dining terrace
07 Façade detail

07

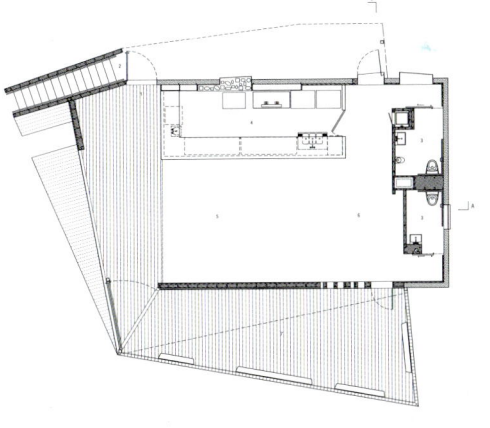

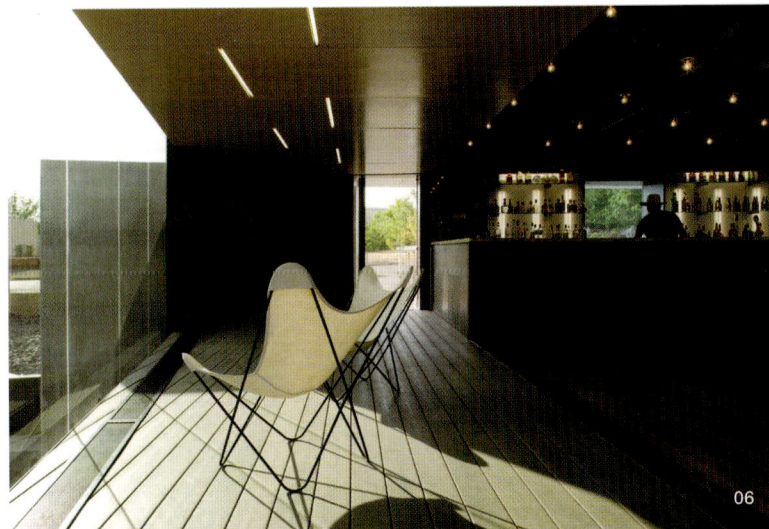

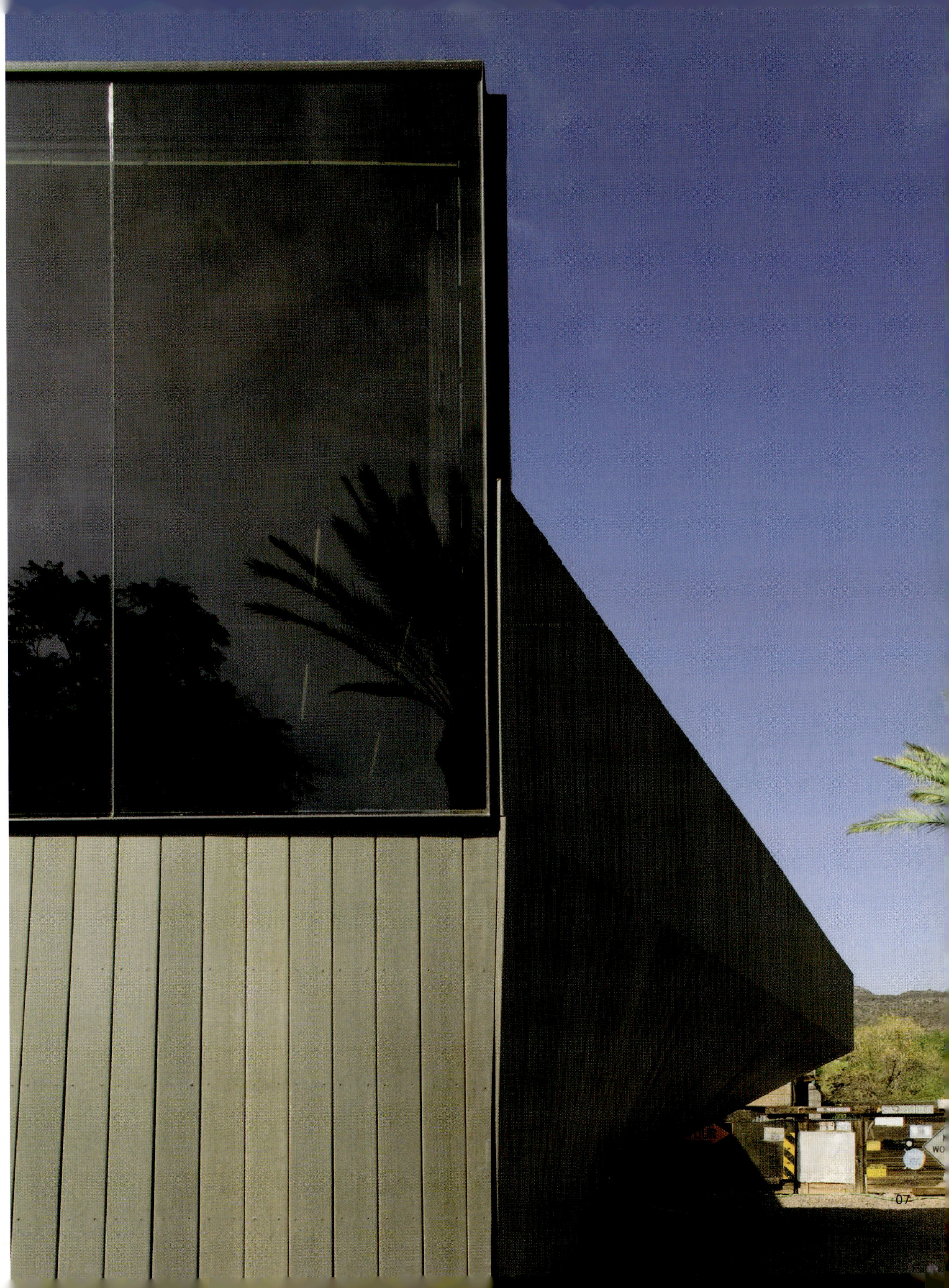

GARCIA RESIDENCE

01

E **The challenge was** to design a structure that would appear to grow out of the rocky desert hillside without dominating the landscape. The house is set on an axis parallel with the site contours, creating three narrow bays that terrace up the hill, allowing excavation to be kept to a minimum. The terracing platforms contain the three zones of the house: living, circulating and sleeping. The entry "gallery" in the middle bay functions as both, circulation and as an extension of the living spaces.

ES **El desafío estaba** en diseñar una estructura que aparecería superar la ladera de desierto rocosa sin dominar el paisaje. La casa se emplaza sobre un eje paralelo con los contornos del solar, creando tres bahías estrechas que forman terrazas en la colina, permitiendo la minima excavación. Las plataformas en los diferentes niveles de las terrazas consisten en las tres zonas de la casa: salas de estar, circulación y habitaciones. La "galería" de entrada en el centro de la bahía funciona como ambos, la circulación y como una extensión de los espacios para habitar.

D **Die Projektaufgabe bestand** darin, einen Wohnbau scheinbar aus dem felsigen Abhang wachsen zu lassen, ohne dabei jedoch die Landschaft zu dominieren. Das Haus steht auf einer Achse, die parallel zu den Rändern des Grundstücks verläuft und dabei drei schmale Buchten formt, die den Berg terrassenartig gliedern. Diese Ebenen umfassen drei Bereiche des Hauses: Wohnen, Bewegung und Schlafen.

F **Le défi consistait** à concevoir une structure qui semblerait sortir des collines rocheuses du désert, sans dominer le paysage. La maison est établie sur un axe parallèle avec les contours du site, créant trois baies étroites qui s'étagent sur la colline, permettant de réduire l'excavation au minimum. Les plateformes en terrasse contiennent les trois zones de la maison : vie, circulation et sommeil. La « galerie » d'entrée dans la baie centrale fonctionne à la fois comme circulation et extension des espaces de vie.

USA

IBARRA ROSANO DESIGN ARCHITECTS

Project City Tucson (AZ)
Typology Living
Completion Year 2001
Photos Bill Timmerman Photography

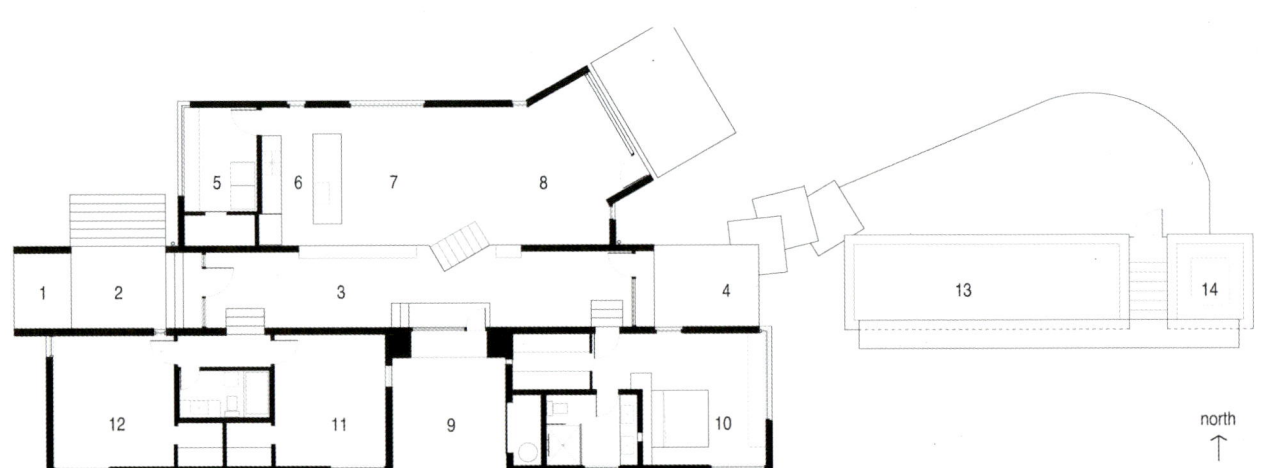

north ↑

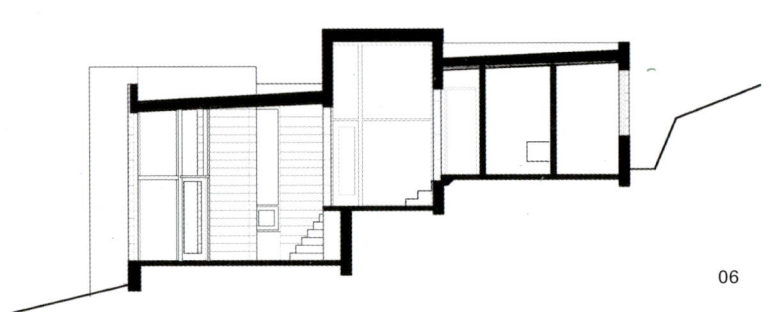

03 Interior
04 Floor plan
05 Rear view by night
06 Longitudinal section

04

07

08

07 Entry detail
08 View of south façade

WINTER RESIDENCE

01

01 Courtyard

E **The owners of** the house wanted to transform their dark, 1940's brick residence into a luminous space reminiscent of the boutique hotels and spas they had visited. The architects took an approach of simplification and reduction. The key to liberating the plan, improving flow and introducing daylight was to remove the bulky fireplace that bisected the living spaces. The interior is now reintegrated with the exterior through courtyards that provide privacy, shelter and frame distant views.

ES **Los propietarios de** la casa quisieron transformar su oscura residencia de ladrillo de los años 40 en un espacio luminoso evocador de los hoteles y spas boutique que habían visitado. Los arquitectos tomaron un acercamiento de simplificación y reducción. La llave a la liberación de la planta, fue el mejoramiento del flujo y la introducción de la luz del día removiendo la chimenea voluminosa que dividia los espacios principales. El interior ahora esta reintegrado con el exterior por medio de los patios que proporcionan la intimidad, refugio y enmarcan vistas distantes.

D **Die Eigentümer wollten** ihr eher düsteres Backsteinhaus aus den 40er Jahren in einen leuchtenden Raum verwandeln, der an heutige Boutique Hotels und Spas erinnern sollte. Die Architekten wählten für die Umsetzung das Konzept von Vereinfachung und Reduktion. Um den Grundriss zu optimieren und mehr Tageslicht zu ermöglichen, wurde der wuchtige Kamin entfernt, der den Wohnbereich in zwei Teile gliederte. Innen und Außen wurden durch Innenhöfe verbunden, welche Ruhe und Sicherheit bieten und Blicke in die Ferne freigeben.

F **Les propriétaires de** la maison voulaient transformer leur résidence en brique des années 40, très sombre, en un espace lumineux rappelant les hôtels boutiques et les spas qu'ils avaient visités. Les architectes ont choisi de suivre une démarche de simplification et de réduction. La clé pour libérer le plan, et en améliorer la fluidité en faisant entrer la lumière du jour, était d'enlever la cheminée encombrante qui divisait en deux les espaces de vue. L'intérieur est à présent réintégré dans l'extérieur grâce à des cours qui offrent de l'intimité et un abri, et encadrent la vue sur le lointain.

USA

IBARRA ROSANO DESIGN ARCHITECTS

Project City Tucson (AZ)
Typology Living
Completion Year 2005
Photos Bill Timmerman Photography

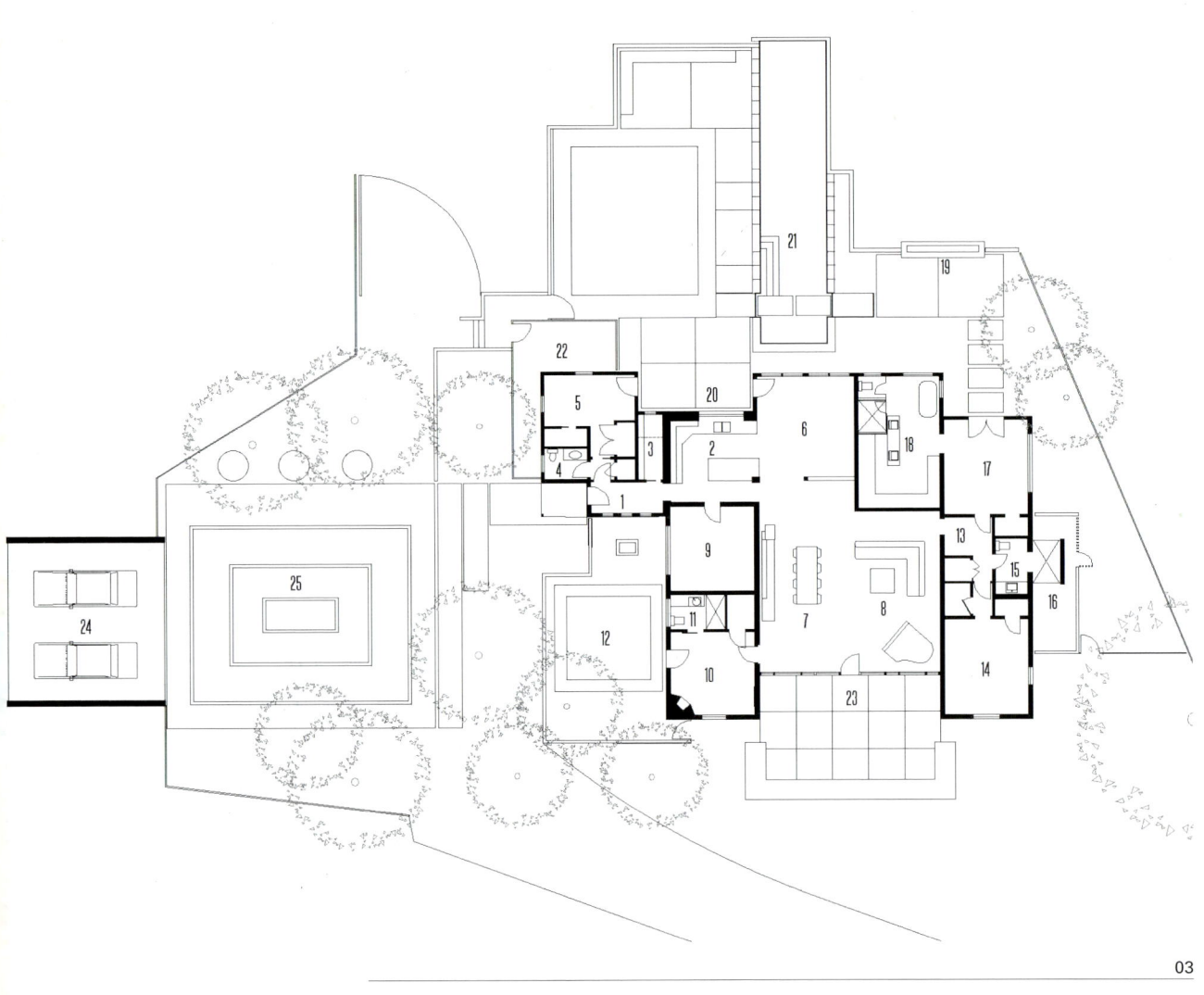

03

04

03 Floor plan
04 Living space with skylight
05 Outdoor area with pool and fireplace
06 Living space with view to city

05

06

MEINEL OPTICAL SCIENCES BUILDING - UNIVERSITY OF ARIZONA

01 Detail of fully glazed façade

E   **The Meinel Optical** Sciences Building is a study of light, where its form is conceived from the Camera Obscura. Within the simple volume, daylight is introduced through a series of apertures, interacting and modulating the spaces within. Three vertical light shafts penetrate the building and terminate in a series of two-story interaction spaces. Each shaft features a specific optical effect rendered in a white veneer plaster, allowing natural daylight to actively integrate into the daily activities of the building.

ES   **El Meinel Optical** Sciences Building es un estudio de luz, donde su forma es concebida de la Cámara Obscura. Dentro del volumen simple, la luz del día es presentada por una serie de aperturas, actuando recíprocamente y modulando los espacios de adentro. Tres ejes verticales ligeras penetran el edificio y se terminan en una serie de espacios de interacción de dos niveles. Cada eje destaca un efecto específico óptico dado en un yeso de chapa blanco, permitiendo a la luz del día natural integrarse en las actividades diarias del edificio.

D   **Das Meinel-Gebäude** ist eine Lichtstudie, die Form an die Camera Obscura angelehnt. In die einfache Bauform dringt Tageslicht durch eine Folge von Blenden, wirkt auf die Räume darin ein und moduliert sie. Drei vertikale Lichtachsen durchdringen das Gebäude und enden in einer Folge von zweigeschossigen Interaktionsbereichen. Jede der Achsen zeigt einen besonderen optischen Effekt; das natürliche Tageslicht wird in die täglichen Aktivitäten des Gebäudes einbezogen.

F   **Le Meinel Building** est une étude sur la lumière, dont la forme s'inspire de la Camera Obscura. Au sein du volume simple, la lumière du jour entre par une série d'ouvertures, qui interagissent et modulent les espaces intérieurs. Trois puits de lumière verticaux pénètrent le bâtiment et s'achèvent dans une série d'espaces d'interaction entre les deux niveaux. Chaque puits crée un effet optique particulier grâce à un plâtre veiné de blanc, permettant à la lumière naturelle de s'intégrer activement dans les activités quotidiennes du bâtiment.

USA
RICHÄRD+BAUER

Project City Tucson (AZ)
Typology Public
Completion Year 2007
Photos Bill Timmerman Photography

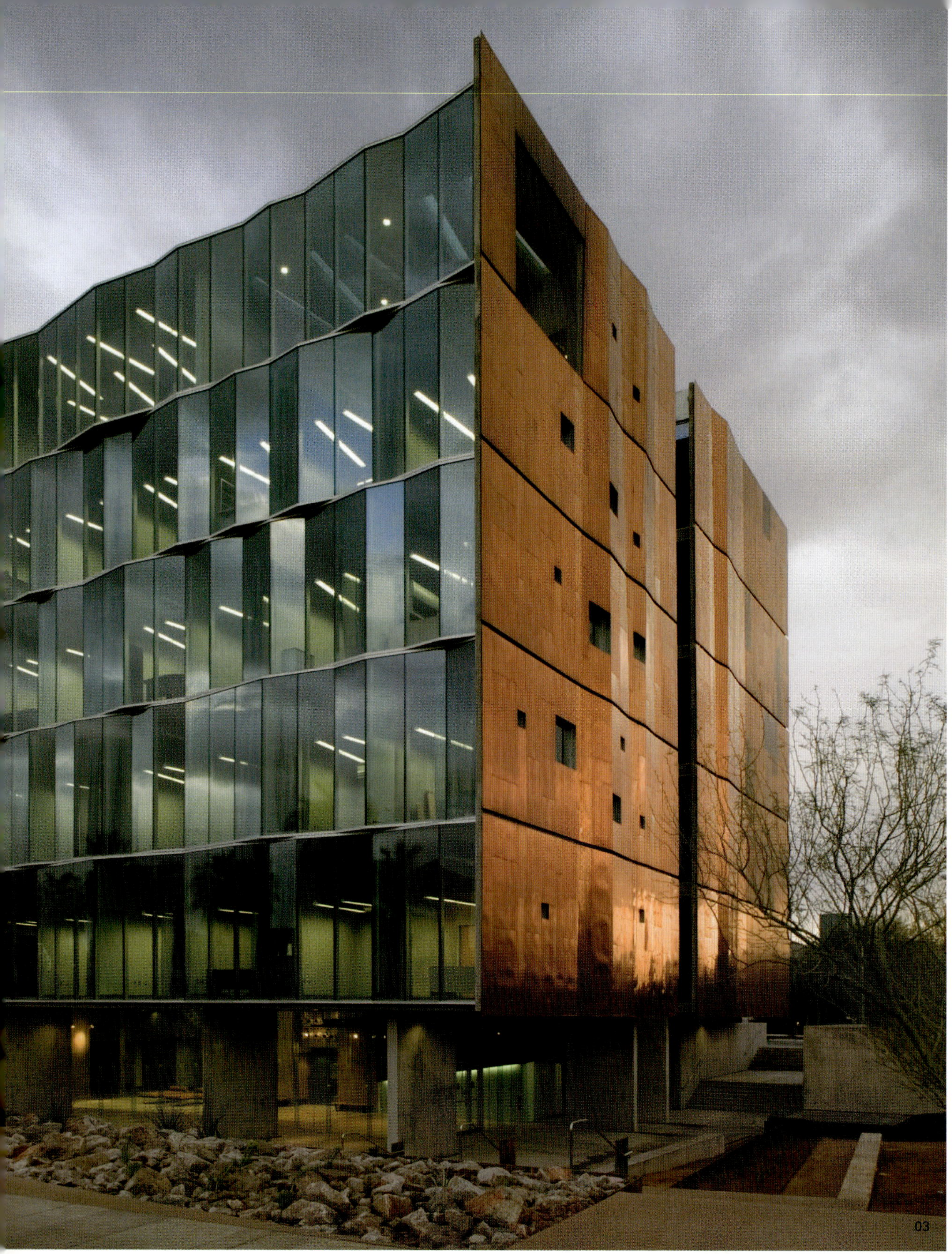

03

03 Glass and copper façade
04 Atrium
05 Sections
06 View into interior

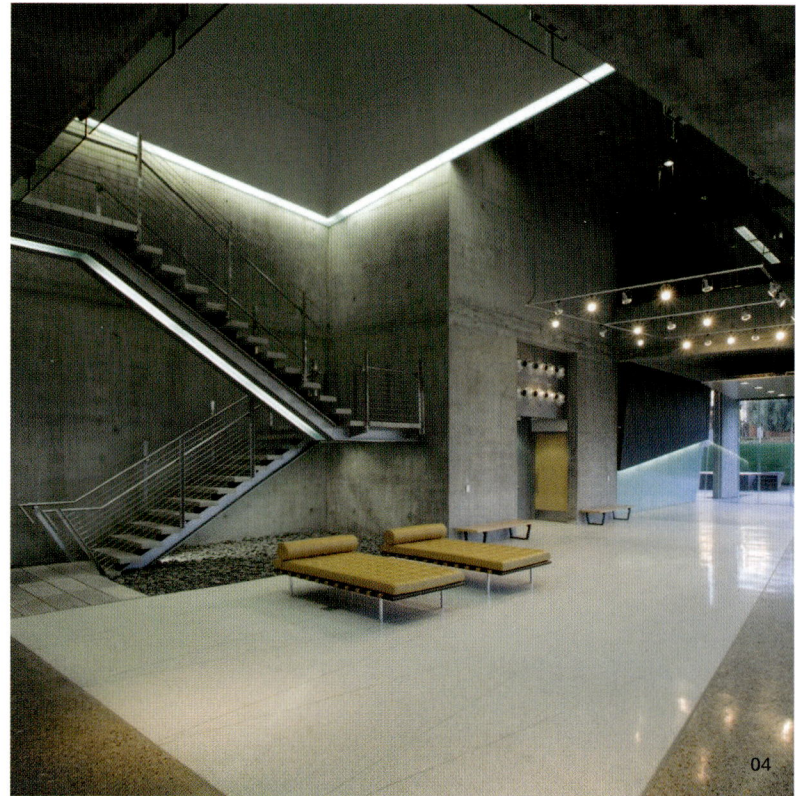

04

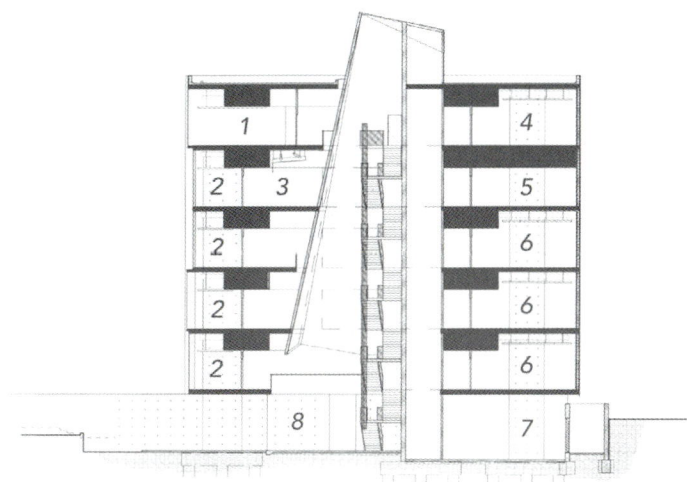

DESERT NOMAD HOUSE

01 House modules in landscape

E   **The three boxes** are nestled in a secluded bowl-like formation in the land, striving for low impact and equilibrium among the saguaros. Divided into three zones, the main living space has an intense early evening view. The setting sun highlights a large craggy rock hill; the low-lying landscape in the foreground is in the shadows of the mountains behind, while the rising sun illuminates a particularly stunning rock face at the top of the mountains. Each box is elevated and one must walk on footpaths between them.

ES   **Las tres ' cajas '** de acero oxidadas estan recostadas individualmente encima de muelles de embarque en una formación aislada parecida a un tazón en el desierto al Oeste de Tucson, esforzandose por impacto minimo y el equilibrio entre los saguaros. Dividido en tres zonas, el espacio principal tiene una vista intensa del atardecer y su interior esta cubierto con el arce pulido. Para circular entre las estructuras, un viajes por el al aire libre caminos llevados en el piso de desierto que teje saguaros altísimo pasado, ocotillos espinoso, y el envainar metálico.

D   **Drei kastenförmige Bauten** schmiegen sich in die Wüstenlandschaft in einer schalenförmigen und abgeschlossenen Formation, behutsam fügen sie sich in die umgebenden Saguaro-Kakteen ein. In drei Bereiche gegliedert, bietet der Hauptwohnbereich am frühen Abend einen beeindruckenden Ausblick. Die Abendsonne beleuchtet einen zerklüfteten Felshügel, während die Morgensonne ein beeindruckendes Felsgesicht auf den Berggipfeln zeichnet. Die drei Kästen wurden leicht erhöht und sind durch Pfade miteinander verbunden.

F   **Les trois boîtes** sont nichées en pleine nature dans une formation reculée en forme de bol, parmi les saguaros, avec un impact minimal sur l'environnement. Divisé en trois zones, l'espace de vie principal offre une vue spectaculaire à l'aube et au crépuscule. Le soleil couchant met en valeur une vaste colline de pierres escarpée, le paysage plus plat au premier plan étant dans l'ombre des montagnes, tandis que le soleil levant illumine la paroi rocheuse particulièrement étonnante au sommet des montagnes. Chaque boîte est surélevée et séparée des autres par un sentier.

USA

RICK JOY ARCHITECTS

Project City Tucson (AZ)
Typology Living
Completion Year 2005
Photos Courtesy Rick Joy Architects

02 View into living/kitchen area from landscape

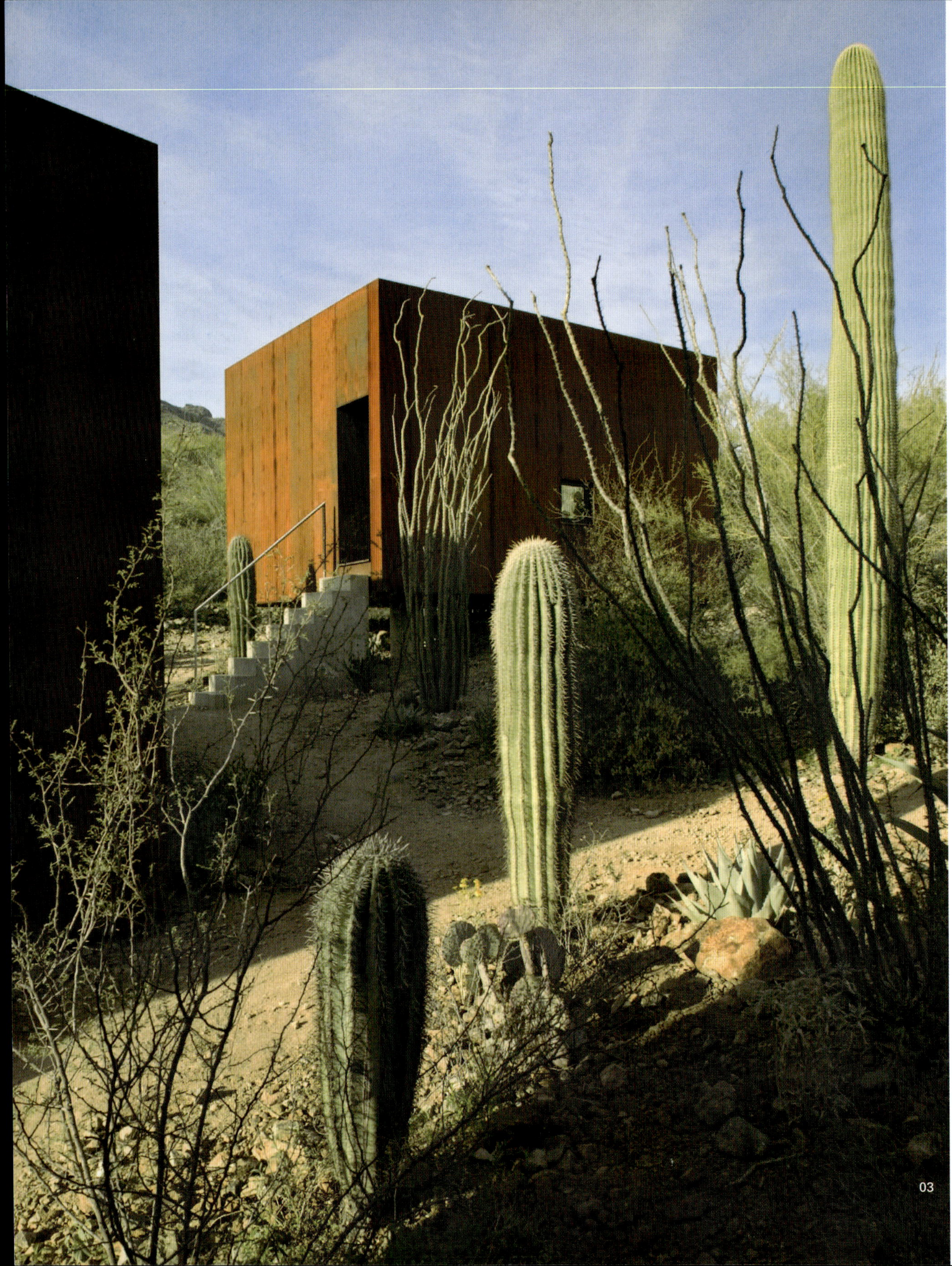

03 Outdoor path between the modules
04 Living room with glass façade
05 Art collection
06 View inside bedroom and bathroom

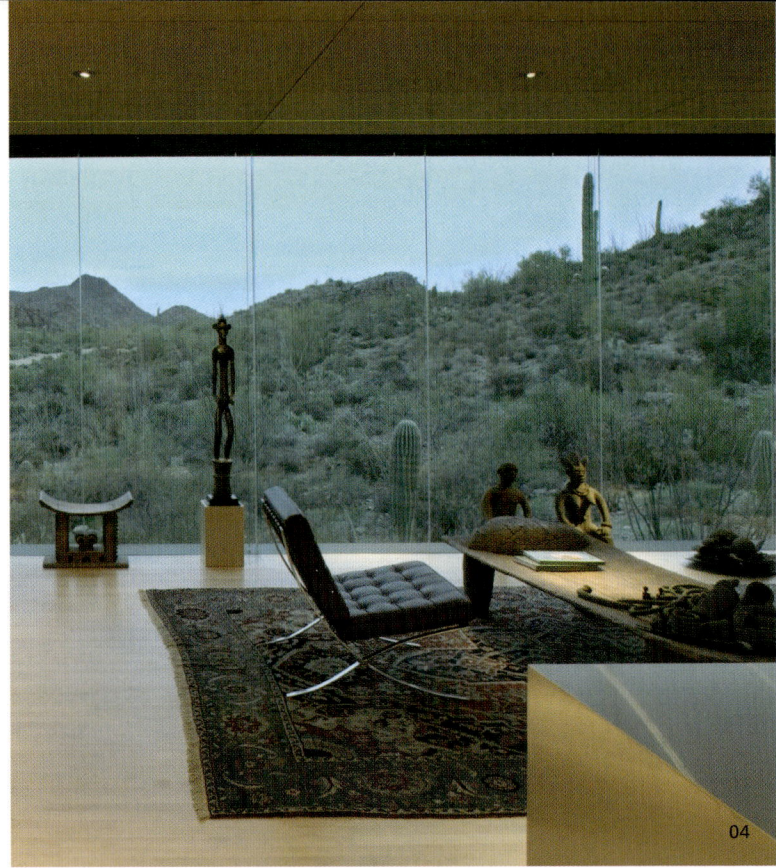

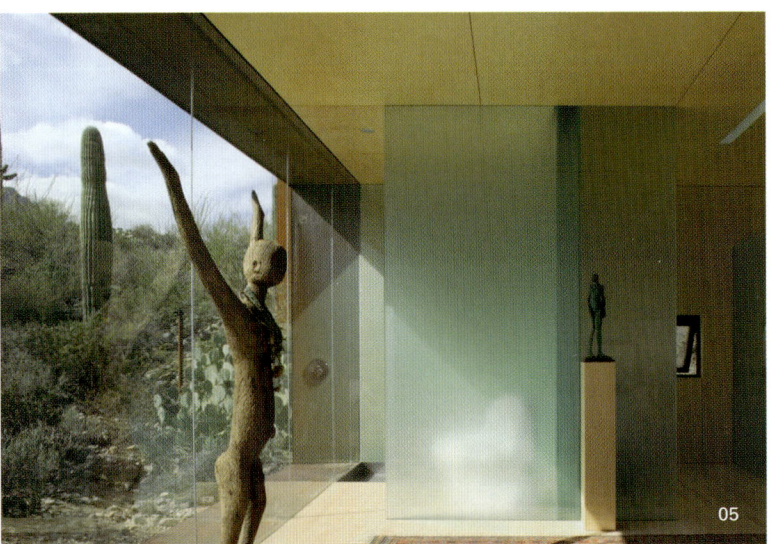

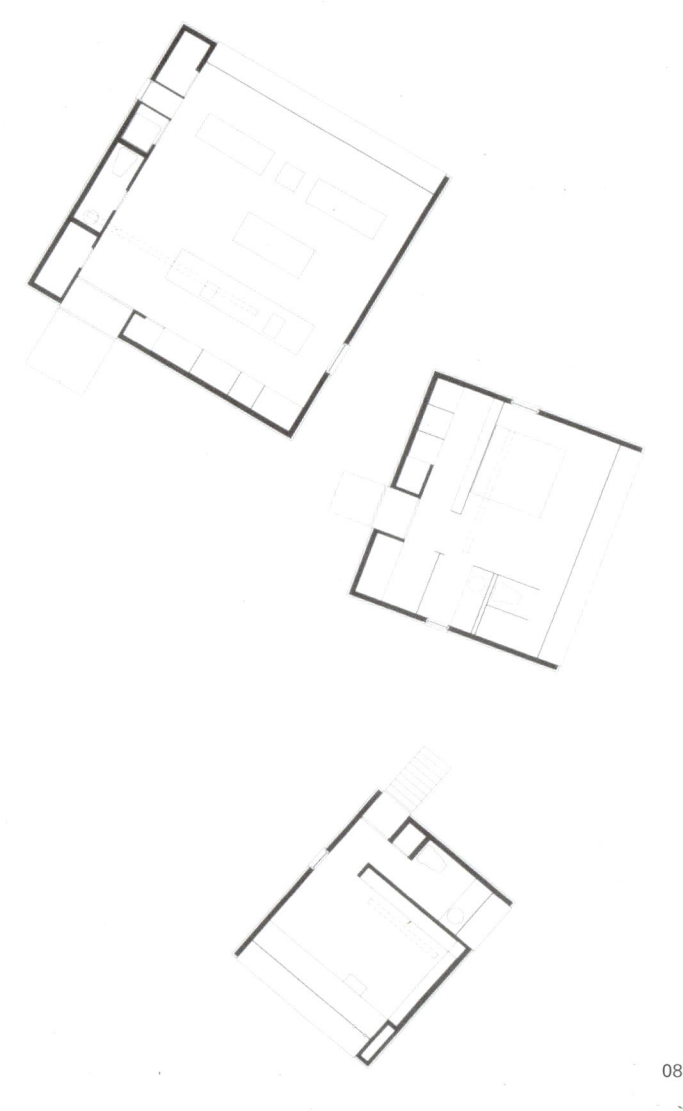

07

08

07 Pathways in between espaces
08 Floor plans
09 Living box nestled in landscape

DESERT PAVILIONS

01   Kitchen/dining area with extended views to courtyard

Situated next to the Saguaro National Park West, seven pavilions are grouped around a historic hacienda, accommodating shared services while providing a sense of communal identity in a remote landscape. Taking advantage of the favorable year-round climate, the outdoors becomes an integral part of the desert lifestyle. The varying clerestory window between the raw, earthen walls and the floating roof, frames views of the surrounding mountains. The pavilions consist of two building masses with distinct outdoor spaces.

ES **Situado al lado** del Oeste de Parque Saguaro Nacional, siete pabellones se agrupan alrededor de una hacienda histórica, acomodando servicios compartidos y al mismo tiempo ofreciendo el sentido de la identidad comunal en un paisaje remoto. Aprovechando el clima favorable durante todo el año, los espacios exteriores se convierten en una parte incorporada del modo de vivir en el desierto. Las diferentes ventanas de claraboya entre las paredes crudas, de tierra y el tejado flotante, enmarca las vistas de las montañas circundantes. Los pabellones consisten en dos volumenes con distintos espacios al aire libre.

D **Direkt neben dem** Saguaro-Nationalpark gruppieren sich sieben Pavillons rund um eine historische Hazienda, die ein Stück gemeinschaftlicher Identität in dieser abgeschiedenen Landschaft stiftet. Das ganzjährig günstige Klima macht die Außenbereiche zu einem integralen Bestandteil des Lebens in der Wüste. Das verstellbare Fenster mit Lichtgaden zwischen den rohen Erdwänden und dem fließenden Dach rahmt den Ausblick auf die umgebenden Berge. Die Pavillons bestehen aus zwei Baukörpern mit klar definierten Außenbereichen.

F **Situés près du** Saguaro National Park West, sept pavillons sont groupés autour d'une hacienda historique, abritant des services d'hébergement partagés tout en procurant un sentiment d'identité commune dans un lieu reculé. Prenant avantage du climat favorable toute l'année, les espaces extérieurs deviennent une partie intégrante de la vie dans le désert. Les différentes ouvertures entre les murs bruts de terre et le toit flottant encadrent la vue sur les montagnes environnantes. Les pavillons consistent en deux masses de bâtiments avec des espaces extérieurs distincts.

USA

RICK JOY ARCHITECTS

Project City Tucson (AZ) – Avra Valley
Typology Living
Completion Year 2010
Renderings Rick Joy Architects

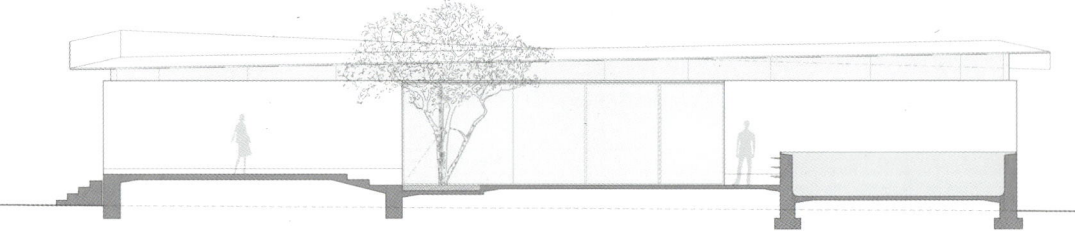

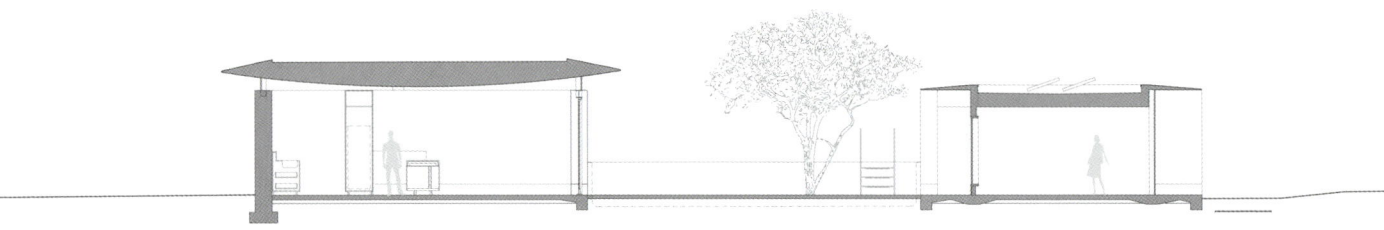

03

04

05

SPACEPORT AMERICA

This project developed support and administrative facilities for Virgin Galactic and the NMSA. Spaces are arranged around external courtyards for daylight penetration and to enhance the opportunity for natural ventilation. Principal operational training functions include a departure lounge, clubhouse, spacesuit dressing rooms, and celebration areas. The canteen and mission control have direct east views across the apron, runway and landscape beyond. The Operational heart of the facility contains a double-height hangar.

ES **Este proyecto desarrollado** consiste de instalaciones administrativas para la empresa Virgen Galactic y el NMSA. Los espacios se organizan alrededor de patios externos para la penetración de luz del día y para mejorar la oportunidad de ventilación natural. Las funciones principales operacionales de entrenamineto, incluyen una sala de embarque, la casa club, vestidores de traje espacial, y salas para celebraciones. La cantina y el centro de control tienen vistas directas de este a través de la pista de aterrizaje y despegue y el paisaje más allá. El nucleo Operacional de la instalación contiene un hangar de altura doble.

D **Das Bauvorhaben umfasst** Versorgungs- und Verwaltungseinrichtungen für Virgin Galactic und die New Mexico Spaceport Authority; das Herz der Anlage ist der doppelgeschossige Hangar. Die Räume gliedern sich um externe Höfe und gewährleisten somit natürliche Belichtung und Belüftung. Die wichtigsten Einrichtungen sind die Abflug-Lounge, ein Clubhaus, Ankleideräume für die Raumanzüge sowie Räume für Festlichkeiten. Die Kantine und das Kontrollzentrum bieten einen direkten Blick über das Vorfeld, die Start- und Landebahn sowie die umgebende Landschaft.

F **Ce projet contient** des installations de soutien technique et d'administration pour Virgin Galactic et la NMSA. Les espaces sont aménagés autours de cours extérieures pour une meilleure pénétration de la lumière du jour et afin d'améliorer la qualité de la ventilation naturelle. Les principales fonctions opérationnelles comprennent un hall de départ, un clubhouse, un vestiaire pour enfiler les combinaisons spatiales, et des espaces festifs. La cantine et la salle de commande jouissent d'une vue directe à l'est sur la zone de trafic, la piste de décollage et le paysage au-delà. Le cœur opérationnel du bâtiment contient un hangar double hauteur.

01   Entry scape

USA
FOSTER + PARTNERS

Project City Upham (NM)
Typology Transportation
Completion Year 2007
Renderings Foster + Partners

03 Exploded building layers
04 Departure lounge
05 West entrance elevation

03

04

05

INDEX

THE OTHER EXTREME: COLD

Michelle Galindo
Ice Architecture
ISBN 978-3-938780-59-6

From the contents
Del contenido
Aus dem Inhalt
Du contenue

■ BOF Architekten: Indian Research Base,
  Larsemann Hills, Arctic
■ Zaha Hadid: Nordpark Cable Railway in Innsbruck,
  Austria
■ schmidt hammer lassen architects: School of
  Nursing and Health Care Practice, Jagtvej,
  Nuuk, Greenland
■ Elenberg Fraser: Huski Hotel in Falls Creek, Victoria,
  Australia
■ Jarmund /Vigsnæs Architects: Svalbard Science Centre
  in Longyearbyen, Norway

EL OTRO EXTREMO: FRIO

DAS ANDERE EXTREM: KÄLTE

L'AUTRE EXTRÊME: FROID

Tana Court, Norway

IMPRINT

The Deutsche Bibliothek is registering this publication in the Deutsche Nationalbibliographie; detailed bibliographical information can be found on the internet at http://dnb.ddb.de

ISBN 978-3-938780-58-9
Copyright 2009 by Verlagshaus Braun
www.verlagshaus-braun.de

1st edition 2009

Editorial staff
Claire Chamot, Franziska Nauck, Sophie Steybe
Edited texts
Eyal Moran
Translations
Spanish introduction: Juan Francisco Lopez
German introduction: Christine Schröter
French texts: Stéphanie Laloix
French introduction: Céline Azzopard
(www.alphagriese.de)
Graphic concept
Kraft plus Wiechmann Grafikdesign